take note

CECILE LEVIN

Maskew Miller Longman

Maskew Miller Longman (Pty) Ltd
Howard Drive, Pinelands. Cape Town

Branches in Johannesburg, Durban, Port Elizabeth, Kimberley,
King William's Town, Pietersburg, Nelspruit, Umtata and Mafikeng,
and representatives throughout southern Africa.

© Maskew Miller Longman (Pty) Ltd 1995

All rights reserved. No part of this publication may be
reproduced. stored in a retrieval system, or transmitted
in any form or by any means, electronic, mechanical,
photocopying, recording, or otherwise, without the
prior written permission of the copyright holder.

First published 1995

ISBN 0 636 01753 2

Edited by Julie-Anne Justus
Book design and typesetting by Beverley Visser
Imagesetting by Castle Graphics
Cover artwork and illustrations by Napier Dunn
Cover reproduction by Den Graphics
Printed by CTP Book Printers, Caxton Street, Parow

To my children

Susan (who thought of the title), Benita and Darrell, who unwittingly provided much of the material during their growing up years.

Children's prayer

Hold my hand, and I'll hold yours
Together we will open new doors
Won't you see the world through our eyes?
Life should be smiles, not tears and sighs.
Let's all pray to Heaven above
Help us make this world full of joy, full of love.

Cecile Levin

Acknowledgements

My thanks to my colleagues and friends for their encouragement and help:

Languages: Issie Fisher (Hebrew); Mpho Kingsley Mothoagae (Sotho and Tswana); Nick Raubenheimer (Zulu); E N Tuswa (Xhosa); the late Pieter Schoeman (Afrikaans).

Editing and practical advice in all aspects of Take Note: Dr Caroline van Niekerk; Margaret Raftery; Debbie Hosking, who also transcribed the songs into solfa.

Typing the first manuscript: Val Smith.

Practical suggestions: Ines Conrad Adams; Saidie Kahn; Miriam Schiff; Sharon Shevil.

Illustrations: Napier Dunn struck 'the right note' with his pencil.

Cassette: Miriam Erasmus, Sharon Katz, Celia Nel and Dawn Selby interpreted the songs with their own individual brand of musicality.

Special thanks . . . to Nell Dachs for sharing her expertise, experience and common sense with characteristic good humour and generosity.

to my husband David and children, for your constant tolerance and enthusiastic support of 'the book'.

Contents

Entries in italic print indicate songs.

Introduction

Singing	ix
Movement	ix
Instruments	x
Accompaniment	x
Poems	x
Speech patterns	x
Names	x
Form	x

Greetings

Shalom	2
Greetings	2
Special words	2
Farewell	3
Thank you	3
Tring-a-ling	4
Ukuvalelisa	4

Getting to know me

Only one mouth	6
Mmele wa ka	6
Net een mond	7
Four eyes	7
The tiger	8
Kunye, kubili, kuthatu	8
Die hanswors	9
Die olifant	10
Ndlovu the elephant	10
The dentist's song	11
Krokodil	11
Die tandarts se lied	12
Open wide	13
Ietermagog	13
Never trust a crocodile	14
Eggbeater	14
An easy remedy	15
Eina! Eina!	15
The snowman	16
The millipede	16
Counting game	17
How to treat a dinosaur	17
Untidy Tim	17
Thola lesea	18

Let's move

Walking song	20
Let's go	20
A longer walk	21
Jabulani the ricksha man	21
Run along	22
Kangaroo	22
Every way	23
Crabs	23
What's in a name?	24
It's not fair	25
Druiwe	26
Galloping	26
Skipping here and skipping there	27
Jumping beans	27
Tjoek-tjoek-tjoek	28
Mntwana uyajabula	29
If I were a bee	29
Astronaut	30
Moths and butterflies	31
Drum beat	31
Umdanso wesicathulo	32
UVusi ugibela ihashi	32
Robala lesea	33

Let's celebrate

Sunday chimes	36
Welcome, Shabbat	37
Yusuf's way	37
Ramadan	37
Diwali	37
Purim – a noisy time	38
Hamantashen	39
Easter bunny	40
Special days and ways	40
Hot cross buns	41
Paasbolletjies	42
Pesach-time	42
Shana tova – happy new year	44
Apples and honey	45
Shavuot	46
Succoth is here!	47
A special birthday	48
Christmas carol	49
Chanukkah	50
My Chanukkah dreidel	51

The seasons

Liyana! Liyana!	54
Winter se liedjie	54
Autumn leaves	55
Granny and the weather	56
Dikgakologo	56
Yiva induduma!	57

	Whatever the weather	57
	Somer is die beste tyd	58
	Herfs	59
	Spring	60
	Ilanga liyashona	61
	Ihlobo lishushu!	62

People and places

	Flower seller's song	64
	Table Mountain	65
	Pietermaritzburg	65
	Namaqualand daisies	66
	Mooi Nomsa	66
	Kirstenbosch se wildeblomtuin	67
	The Indian Market	67
	Diamond digging	68
	Sugar	68
	Grape fun!	69
	What is a raisin?	69

All kinds of creatures

	Hoopoe	72
	Piet-my-vrou	72
	Die hadeda	73
	Bird talk	74
	Peculiar birds	74
	Kokkewiet se lied	75
	Penguin	75
	Volstruis	76
	Fruit bat	76
	Isikhukhukazi	76
	Iinyosi	76
	Spider	77
	Snakes	77
	Coelacanth	78
	No place for a fish	79
	Lady Dimple	79
	The whale	80
	The Kruger National Park	81
	Die nagapie	82
	Silkworm time!	83
	Hyenas	84
	Dintja tsa me	84
	Ratel	85
	Rhinoceros	85
	Zebra	86

Musical concepts

	Stop streets	88
	Traffic lights	89
	Verkeersligte	89
	The postbox	90
	Why can't I?	90

Mole	91
Up and down the xylophone ladder	92
Gardening	92
Lala kahle	93
Avocado pears	94
Cheetah	94
The ostrich	95
Postman's song	96
Our snail	97
Hasie en skilpad	97
Gijima! Gijima!	97
Trains	98
Horses	99
A squirrel's life	100
Slang	101
Porcupine	102
Thula mntwana	103
Lala sana	104
The bulldozer's song	104
Tsoha! Tsoha!	105

Glossary

Musical terms and signs	106
Dynamics	106
Form	106

Music theory

Major scales	107
Harmonic minor scales	108
Pentatonic scale	109
Guitar chords	110

Introduction

The songs, poems and speech patterns in this book have been designed to encourage and stimulate young children in their early encounters with music.

Teachers and parents of young children should develop their own ideas based on the material in this book. Children's ideas should be incorporated too.

Some general teaching tips which will help to make the most of *Take Note* include:

Singing

Practise the song before the lesson so that you can sing it confidently with accurate pitch, accurate rhythm and clear diction.

Indicate with a definite nod or hand movement when the children are to begin.

Play the starting note on a tuned piano, guitar or xylophone to ensure that you start singing on the correct note. If you do not have an instrument, establish your own 'doh' and find the starting note from there. Play or sing the starting note before the children sing so that they become used to accurate pitch. A tuning fork is useful for establishing accurate pitch.

Children should sing and play instruments within the range of fairly loud to very soft. Interpret *f* as fairly loud and *p* as very soft when applied to children. Voices will then remain free of strain and instruments will remain intact.

Do not equate shouting with good singing as in 'Let's hear who can sing the loudest!' Children have enough practice shouting on the playground and playing fields.

Movement

Practise moving and clapping so that you can do so confidently in the classroom.

Children respond to the clear sound of a drum beat or hand clap. Practise walking while clapping and saying 'walk walk', or running while clapping and saying 'run-ning run-ning' so that you can do so confidently for the children.

The children must listen to the beat before they can move with it.

Adjust the speed of the beat to that of the children's step. Children generally walk and run at a faster speed than adults do.

Instruments

All instruments, whether home-made, basic or luxury, must be treated with care and respect.

The children should practise picking up and putting down beaters and instruments quietly.

Instruments suggested in *Take Note* are interchangeable within the same family. For example, you can use a xylophone, chime bars or glockenspiel for melody, and a drum, woodblock or claves for pulse or special effects.

Useful classroom instruments include:

Melodic: chime bars, xylophone, glockenspiel, glasses filled with water. The alto xylophone should be used rather than the soprano as it is closer to the children's vocal range. Two children may play an ostinato on one xylophone.

Non-melodic: hand drum, drums, tambourines, cymbals, woodblocks, claves, maracas, bells, hand bells. If you do not have any instruments, use body percussion, speech or vocal sounds. Make simple instruments in class. They will be treated with the greatest respect in the music lesson!

Accompaniment

The song is important. The accompaniment adds colour but must not 'drown' the song. Only a few instruments are needed. The class can be divided into several groups: one to sing, one to play the accompaniment and one to act out the song. In this way, all children can be involved in the performance of one song.

Speech patterns

These are rhythmic speech patterns used to develop the child's natural rhythmic ability. Use body percussion to establish the pulse and the pattern. Transfer the body percussion activities to instruments. Use the speech pattern rhythms as accompaniments to songs and poems.

Poems

Introduce the poem with a rhythmic pattern (introduction) developed from the natural beat of the poem and a speech pattern from the poem. Use the same pattern as a link between verses, and as an ending (coda) after the poem.

Names

Personalise the songs and poems by replacing names with the names of children in your class.

Form

The children can experience form by listening to songs and poems, and deciding whether they show repetition or contrast. Encourage children to make relevant graphic representations, such as   A   B   A
                △ △ △

Greetings

SHALOM
(Hebrew)

A happy song
Doh: F (Key: D minor)

Sha-lom we greet when we meet, Sha-lom we cry when we wave "Good-bye!"

Sha-lom means peace be with you wher-e-ver you go, what-e-ver you do!

Children clap and say the words, then clap and sing the song.

A song and dance for *Shalom*

The children form pairs, find their own space and face each other.

Bars 1 and 2   Shake hands.
Bars 3 and 4   Wave.
Bars 5 to 8   Link arms, skip around in 'tiekie-draai' style.

Greetings (Zulu, Hebrew, Afrikaans)

Sawubona, Sipho! Usaphila na?
Shalom, Rachel! Ma shlomcha?
Hallo, Sue! How are you?
Môre Nico! Hoe gaan dit met jou?

Children say and clap each greeting. The teacher may say a greeting and the children echo-clap the rhythm. These activities may be done individually or in groups.

Children can also form a circle. One child stands inside the circle. At each greeting he or she moves to shake hands with a different child. Older children may all move one step to the right or left, so that the child in the middle meets a new one without moving.

Special words (Zulu, Xhosa, Tswana)

Uxolo, nceda, tsweetswee, please
Important words that mean a lot –
As easy as a sneeze!

FAREWELL
(Zulu, Afrikaans, Hebrew)

Doh: G (Key: E minor)

p Sa- la ka- hle, tot- siens, Sha- lom, good- bye. When we wave fare- well there's a tear in my eye.

mf We've had fun to- ge- ther, friends in e - v'ry way! I'll miss you more than words can e - ver say.

slower and softer

Accompaniment (xylophone)

good - bye

THANK YOU
(Xhosa, Zulu, Afrikaans)

Thank you, en- ko- si, ngiya- bo- nga, dan- kie. Spe- cial words from peo- ple of our coun- try.

🎓 *Establish the ♩ pulse by snapping or clapping ♩ ♩ ♩ throughout the speech pattern. Start one bar before the children say the rhyme and finish one bar after the rhyme is completed.*

Tring-a-ling

Tring-a-ling, tring-a-ling
Are you at home?
I'm calling you
On the telephone!

Tring-a-ling, tring-a-ling
Oh! Answer, do!
There's something that
I MUST tell you!

Tring-a-ling, tring-a-ling
There's still no reply!
I'll try again later –
Totsiens[1], goodbye!

(a short pause)

Tring-a-ling, tring-a-ling
Hullo! At last!
Chubby's had puppies![2]
Come over, fast!

[1] Substitute other languages.
[2] Encourage the children to make up a reason for the call. Combine this poem with the children's 'News Time'.

The children will enjoy ringing a hand bell or playing the triangle during the 'tring-a-lings'.

Ukuvalelisa
(Zulu)

Hamba kahle
Sobuye sibonane
Unyembezi ehlweni lami.

Goodbye
(Translated from Zulu)

Goodbye
Until we meet again
There's a tear in my eye.

Introduction and coda

Clap ♩ ♩ ♩ ♩ before and after the poem.
     Ham - ba kah - le

Getting to know me

ONLY ONE MOUTH

At a steady pace
Doh: D (Key: D major)

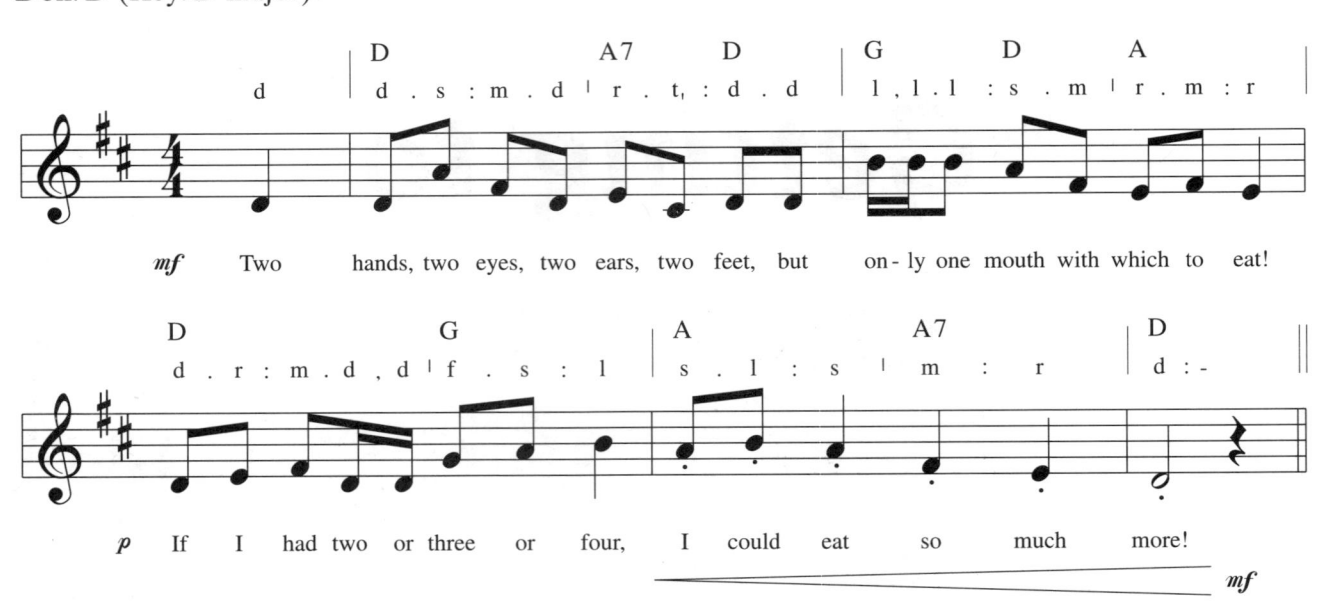

mf Two hands, two eyes, two ears, two feet, but on-ly one mouth with which to eat!

p If I had two or three or four, I could eat so much more! —— *mf*

A fun poem for learning parts of the body. A child meets her grandfather and asks him where he has been. He answers that he has come from the doctor – and that he has aches and pains in the following parts of his body.

Mmele wa ka
(Sesotho traditional)

Hloho
Nko
Le molomo
Mahetla
Sefuba
Le letheka
Mangoele
Le menwana

My body
(Translated from Sesotho)

Head
Nose
And mouth
Shoulders
Chest
And waist
Knees
And toes

NET EEN MOND
(Afrikaans)

Doh: C (Key: C major)

```
    |C              |G              |C              |G            |
    s   m : d  : s  | f  : r  : s   | m  : d  : m   | r : - : -   |
```

p Twee o - ë, twee o - re. Maar slegs net een mond!

```
    |C              |Dm             |G              |C            |
    d : r : m       | r : m.m : f   | s : s : s     | m : d : d   :||
```

Waar - om nie twee drie of vier? Dan eet ek so - veel meer!

f

Four eyes

Into the kitchen
I quietly creep.
No one's around,
I'm sure Mom's asleep!

Carefully I open
The biscuit jar
I take one out
And THERE YOU ARE!

Mom, were you joking
When you said
You have two eyes
At the BACK of your head?

I've looked and looked
As hard as can be,
But TWO in FRONT
Are all I can see!

🎓 *Choose a rhythmic pattern from the poem to use as the introduction, accompaniment, link between verses and coda (additional ending).*

e.g. pat ♩♩ ♩ ♩ 𝄽

qui - et - ly creep

7

THE TIGER

Doh: G (Key: G major)

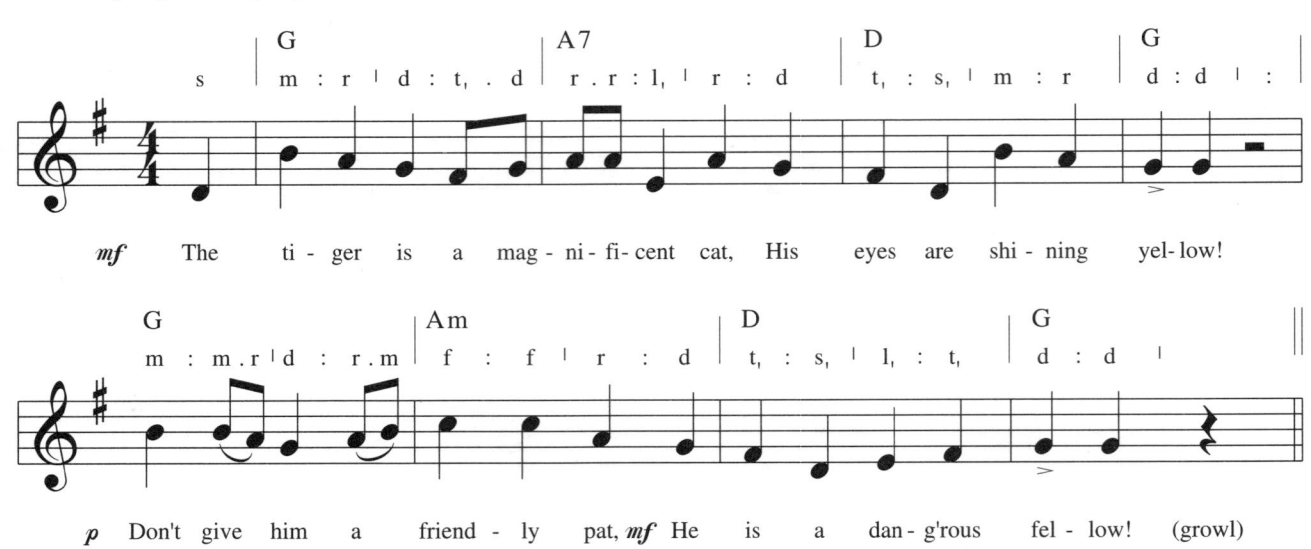

mf The tiger is a magnificent cat, His eyes are shining yellow!

p Don't give him a friendly pat, *mf* He is a dang'rous fellow! (growl)

Accompaniment (drum)

Bar 4   Drum   ‡ ‡ ♩ ♩
                1 2 ye-llow

Let's be ... TIGERS

Children make yellow masks from cardboard.
The 'tigers' move on all-fours, preen themselves, bare their teeth and show their 'claws' at the appropriate words.

Tell the children that ...

A semi-precious stone found in South Africa and Namibia is called a 'tiger's eye' because it is brown with shiny yellow flecks.

A poem with a definite rhythmic beat. The translation provides another poem!

Kunye, kubili, kuthathu
(Zulu traditional)

Kunye, kubili, kuthathu
Mama bambile lozenze
Zenze yifile, Mama khalile,
Kunye, kubili, kuthathu.

One, two, three
(Translated from Zulu)

One, two, three,
Mother caught a flea,
Flea died, Mother cried,
One, two, three!

A song to make us smile.

DIE HANSWORS
(Afrikaans)

With a flowing rhythm
Doh: F (Key: F major)

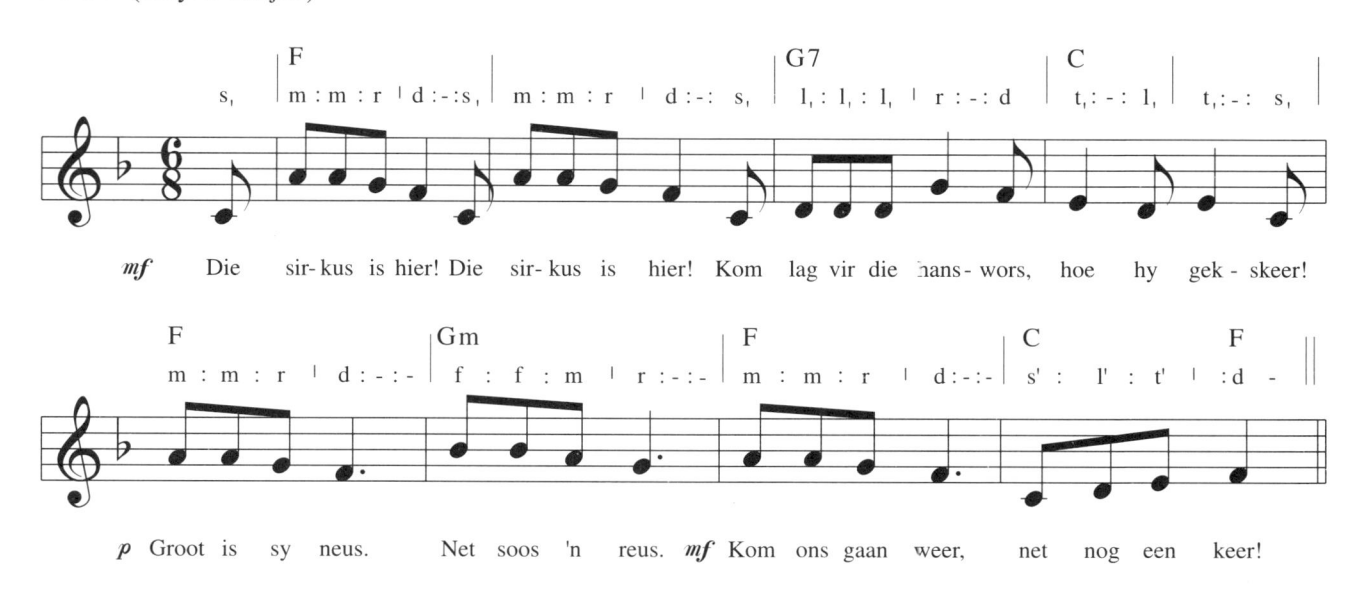

mf Die sir-kus is hier! Die sir-kus is hier! Kom lag vir die hans-wors, hoe hy gek-skeer!

p Groot is sy neus. Net soos 'n reus. *mf* Kom ons gaan weer, net nog een keer!

Verse 2
Die sirkus is hier! Die sirkus is hier!
Kom lag vir die hanswors, hoe hy gekskeer!
Wange so rond, klere so bont!
Kom ons gaan weer, net nog een keer!

Accompaniment (tambourine, triangle)

Tambourine ♪ 𝄾 𝄾 ♪ 𝄾 𝄾 throughout.
            gaan   weer

Bars 5 and 6   △ ♪ 𝄾 𝄾 ♫♫
               kom   kom ons gaan

A song and dance with *Die Hanswors*

Form a circle.

Bars 1 to 4, 7 and 8   Face the right, skip to the right.
Bars 5 and 6   Stand, point at the appropriate part of the body and act the words.

DIE OLIFANT
(Afrikaans)

Doh: F (Key: D minor)

Dm	Gm	Dm	A7	Dm	A
l, : d : m	l, : d : m	f : r : f	m : - : d	r : r : t,	d : - : l,	t, : m : re	m : - : m

mf Kyk na die o - li - fant van el - ke kant! Met o - re so groot, en slurp so lank! Sy
f

Dm	Gm	A7	Dm	A7	Dm
l : l : s	f : - : m	r : r : d	t, : - : t,	m : - : f	m : - : r	d : : t,	l, : - : -

stert - jie net soos 'n kru - lle - tjie klein. Dit lyk as - of dit sal ver - dwyn!
p

Let's be... ELEPHANTS

Bar 3   Place index fingers above ears, elbows out, making elephants' ears with your arms.

Bar 4   Place both outstretched arms in front, hands touching to make a 'trunk'.

Bars 5 to 8   Place wrist where tail would be! Flap the wrist and wriggle the fingers.

Ndlovu the elephant

Ndlovu's ears
Are as big as this.
He's an animal
You CANNOT miss!

His long grey trunk
Is a useful device –
Wouldn't you buy one
At ANY price?

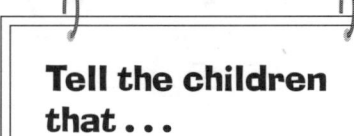

Tell the children that...

Ndlovu is a Zulu name for an elephant, just as Jumbo is an English name for one.

Introduction, accompaniment, link and coda

Clap   use - ful de - vice

THE DENTIST'S SONG

Walking song
Doh: C (Key: C major)

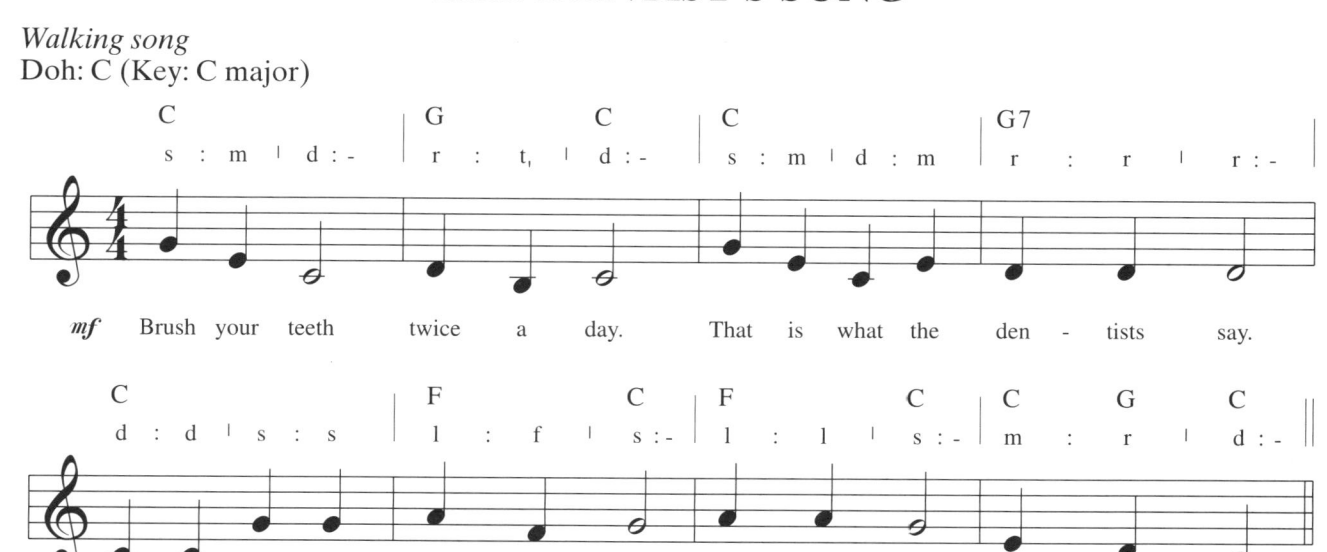

| C | G | C | C | G7 |
| s : m | d : - | r : t, | d : - | s : m | d : m | r : r | r : - |

mf Brush your teeth twice a day. That is what the den - tists say.

| C | F | C | F | C | C | G | C |
| d : d | s : s | l : f | s : - | l : l | s : - | m : r | d : - |

Down and up, on top be - low. Brush them well! Here we go!

KROKODIL

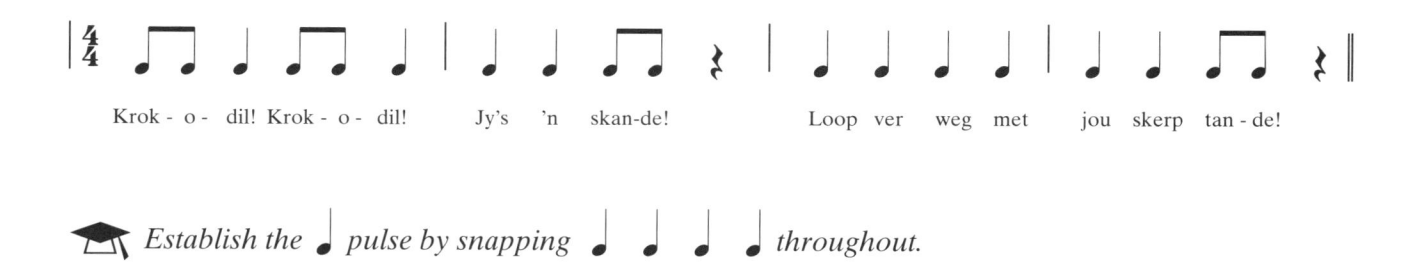

Krok - o - dil! Krok - o - dil! Jy's 'n skan - de! Loop ver weg met jou skerp tan - de!

🎓 *Establish the ♩ pulse by snapping ♩ ♩ ♩ ♩ throughout.*

Accompaniment

Group A: kro - ko - dil / kro - ko - dil
pat pat clap / pat pat clap

Group B: stamp ⁄ snap ⁄

Let's be ... CROCODILES

Children sit in a circle with one child, the 'crocodile', in the middle. They act the words, pointing at the crocodile, who finally runs out of the circle.

DIE TANDARTS SE LIED
(Afrikaans)

Doh: F (Key: F major)

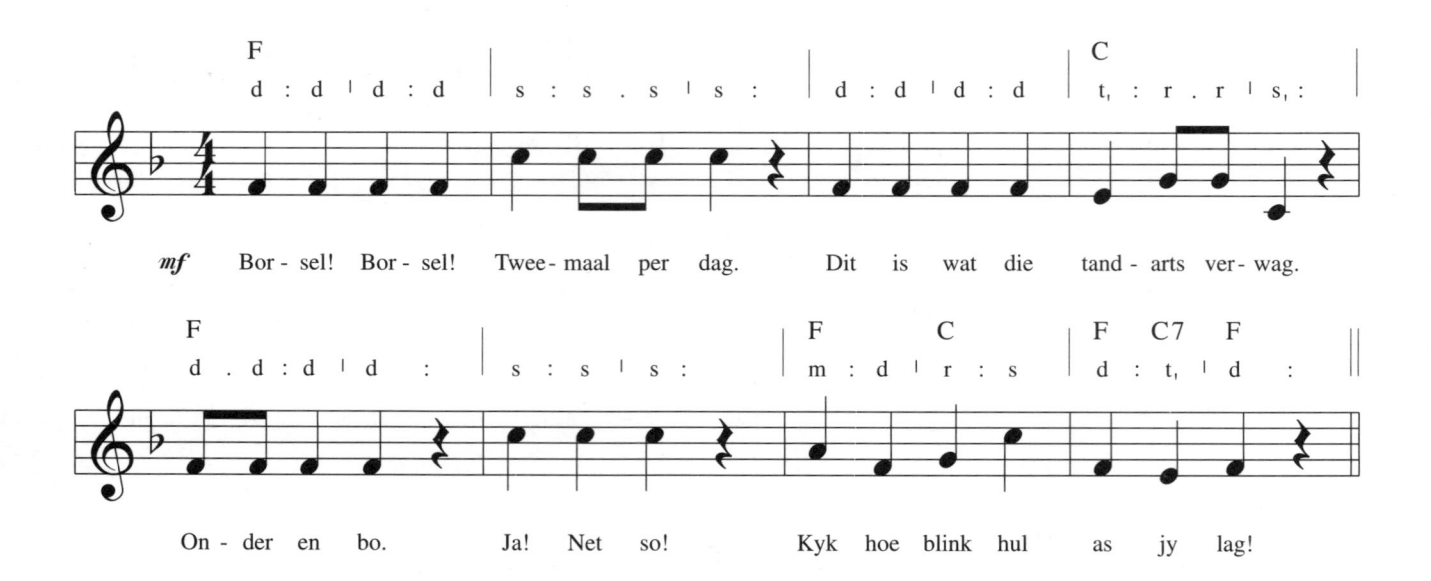

```
  F                                              C
  d : d | d : d  | s : s . s | s : s :  | d : d | d : d  | t, : r . r | s, :
```

mf Bor - sel! Bor - sel! Twee - maal per dag. Dit is wat die tand - arts ver - wag.

```
  F                                              F      C     F    C7   F
  d . d : d | d :   | s : s | s :    | m : d | r : s | d : t, | d :
```

On - der en bo. Ja! Net so! Kyk hoe blink hul as jy lag!

Introduction, accompaniment and coda

on - der en bo

clap clap clap stamp

Let's . . . BRUSH OUR TEETH

1. Right hand imitates the down-up movement in time to the pulse. Then it is the left hand's turn.
2. Now do the down-up in a circular movement, as if brushing teeth.
3. Slide palms across each other in time to the pulse.

OPEN WIDE

A happy song
Doh: C (Key: C major)

mf Mother tells our baby to "open wide!" Then she puts the spoon with food right inside! I'm glad I'm not a baby and can feed myself! I can even reach the cookies on the highest shelf! (Fingers on lips) Oh yes!

L L R R L

A song and dance to *Open Wide*

Children form a circle.

Bars 1 to 12	Run to the right.
Bars 13 to 16	Stand, clap the pulse.
Bars 17 and 18	When the melody is played on a xylophone, the singers place their fingers on their lips. All then shout out, 'Oh yes!'

It's not often that children are asked to stick out their tongues!

Ietermagog *(Afrikaans)*

Ietermagog,
Eienaardige dier!
Sy lang tong vang
Die kleinste mier.
Sy skubbe beskerm hom
Teen enige skade
Want die ander diere
Kom nie nader . . .

Let's be . . . ANTEATERS

Sit or stand in a circle. One child, 'the ietermagog', is in the middle and acts the words of the first verse while the teacher or class says the poem.

Verse 2
The circle moves backwards.

Never trust a crocodile

Never trust a crocodile.
His tears are false,
So's his smile –

His teeth are as sharp as can be!
Don't go near
When he's angry!

He's not the sort that you should stroke, (stroke your arm)
'Cos playing with him
May not be a joke!

> ### Let's be . . . CROCODILES again
> Children place their arms in front of them, open at a 'scissor' angle, and close them with a loud clap at the end of the poem.

A poem for rolling the Rs.

Eggbeater

Whirr-whirr
That's the sound
Of our eggbeater whirrr-ing
Round and round.

Mummy's hand
Must be sore,
But still she goes whirr-ing
More and more.

Whirr-whirr!
Sounds good to me!
I think we're having
Cake for tea!

Children move their hands in a clockwise and then anti-clockwise direction. Tambourines and shakers make a 'whirr-ing' sound, less dangerous than a hand beater.

AN EASY REMEDY

With much feeling
Doh: F (Key: F major)

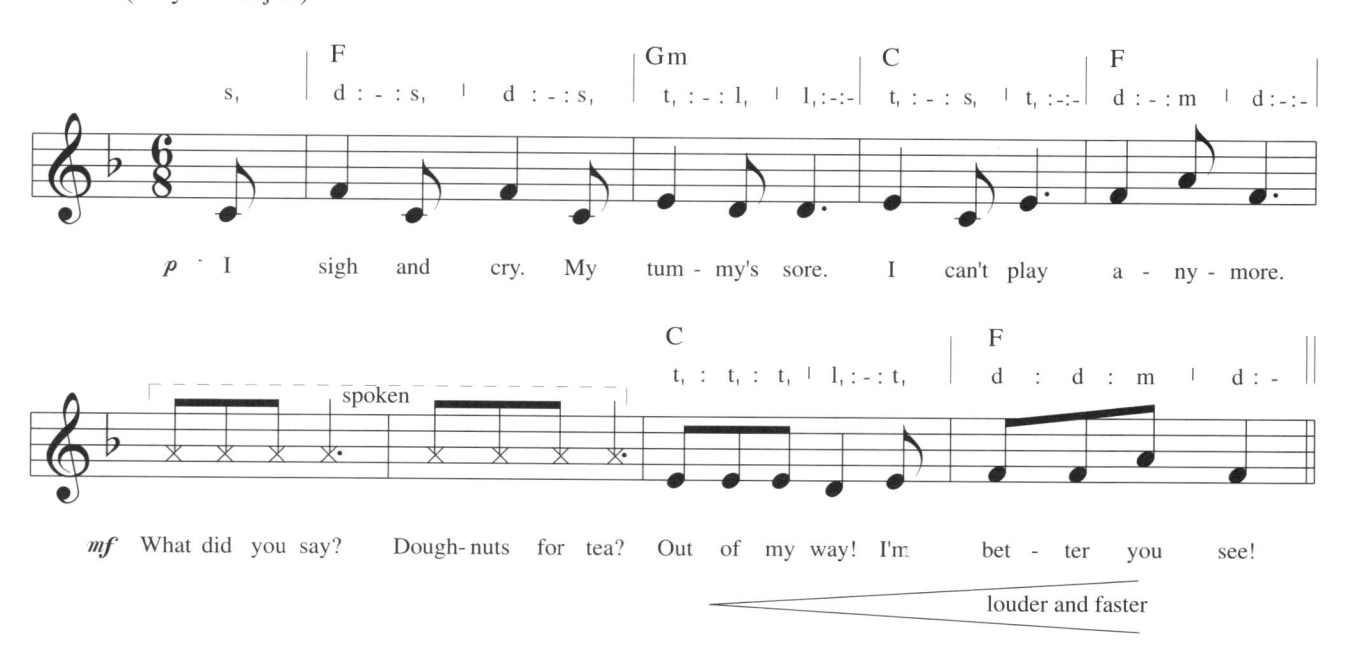

p I sigh and cry. My tum-my's sore. I can't play a-ny-more.

mf What did you say? Dough-nuts for tea? Out of my way! I'm bet-ter you see!

louder and faster

🎓 *Encourage the children to suggest their own favourite food, instead of doughnuts.*

Accompaniment (claves)

Dough-nuts for tea? throughout.

Eina! Eina! *(Afrikaans)*

Eina! Eina!
Kom gou hier!
Ek voel naar,
My maag is seer.

Sussie! Sussie!
Hoe sê jy?
Koeksusters[1] vir tee?
Die pyn is verby!

[1] Encourage the children to suggest their own favourite food.

THE SNOWMAN

Rhythmically
Doh: F (Key: F major)

p I wonder how my snowman felt when the sun came out and he began to melt!

mf First the hands and then the head! Where my snowman stood there's water instead!

Sound effects

| C | D | E | F | G | A | B♭ | C |

End the song with a descending glissando played on the glockenspiel.

Let's be ... SNOWMEN

Children stand upright, then gradually flop down onto the floor, like melting snowmen.

The millipede

The millipede
Has a problem indeed.
He has so many legs!
Oh yes! He grows
More legs, more legs,
Until at last
'No more!' he begs!

Tell the children that ...

The South African name for a millipede is a songololo or shongololo. (See page 24.)

Extend the poem by calling on as many children as you wish to say 'more legs'. This method makes the class alert as they wonder whose turn will be next.

The teacher must use eye contact and show the children with facial expression and/or hands when he or she is ready for the last two lines.

Counting game

1 - 2 - 3 - 4
All sit on the floor!

5 - 6 - 7 - 8
Stand up, very straight!

9 - 10, Now then,
Sit down and start again!

For children who fear that this popular but frightening creature might appear at their front door.

How to treat a dinosaur

Knock-knock!
Who's that at the door?
Dino-Dino-Dinosaur!

If I saw
A dinosaur
Standing outside my front door,
I wouldn't scream! I wouldn't roar!
I would gently
Shake his paw.

I'd say, Brontosaurus!
Come with me
And meet all my family.
Mom would scream! Dad would roar!
But I would gently
Shake his paw.

A poem with a moral!

Untidy Tim

Tim can't find his cricket bat
Tim can't find his furry hat
Tim can't find his brand new shoes
What else will Tim lose?

The hat is lying on the floor
The shoes are outside his front door
The bat? Where's that? Oh, surely not!
It's growing in the flower pot!

Tim must learn the Golden Rule
When he comes home from school
Put clothes and toys straight away
In their places, every day.

Then Tim will find his cricket bat
Tim will find his furry hat
Tim will find his brand new shoes
Nothing more will Tim lose!

THOLA LESEA
(Sesotho)

Doh: F (Key: F major)

F	C	F	C	F	Gm	C	F

s : m : s | f : r : f | m : d : m | r : - : s, | d : - : m | r : - : f | s : s : m | d : d :

Tho- la le - se - a! Ma - me - la. Ma - me - la Mme oa bi - na Tho- la - le - se - a.

Sleep, my baby *(Translated from Sesotho)*

Sleep my baby
Listen! Listen!
Mother is singing,
Sleep, my baby.

Let's move

This song may be used to introduce other songs of the children's choice.

WALKING SONG

Doh: C (Key: C major)

```
   C              | F               | G               | C              ||
   s : m  | s : m | f : l  | l  : l | s : s  | l  : t | d' : s | d' :   ||
```

mf Walk! Walk! Walk! Walk! down the street. We've lots of friends to meet and greet!

🎓 *The teacher plays the ♩ pulse on the hand drum. The children sing, clap the ♩ pulse and walk around the room. Repeat the song several times to give the children practice in walking in time to the hand drum.*

LET'S GO

Walk! Walk! This is fun! Wait un-til we start to run. Skip-ping, hop-ping, jump-ing too. We look as if we're at the zoo.

Accompaniment (1)

Divide the class into three groups. The teacher or a child says the pattern, and the class provides the ♩ pulse accompaniment.

Group A   Bar 1 stamp or drums
Group B   Bar 2 clap or claves
Group C   Bars 3 and 4 pat or ∆

Accompaniment (2)

Each group does their body percussion separately, then together.

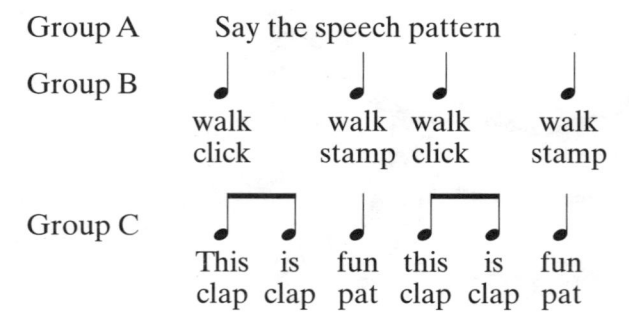

Group A   Say the speech pattern

Group B
    walk   walk   walk   walk
    click   stamp   click   stamp

Group C
    This is   fun   this is   fun
    clap clap   pat   clap clap   pat

Playing a-round

Make the pattern into a round. Group B starts the pattern when group A reaches bar 3. They will complete the round two bars after group A has finished.

A LONGER WALK

Doh: C (Key: C major)

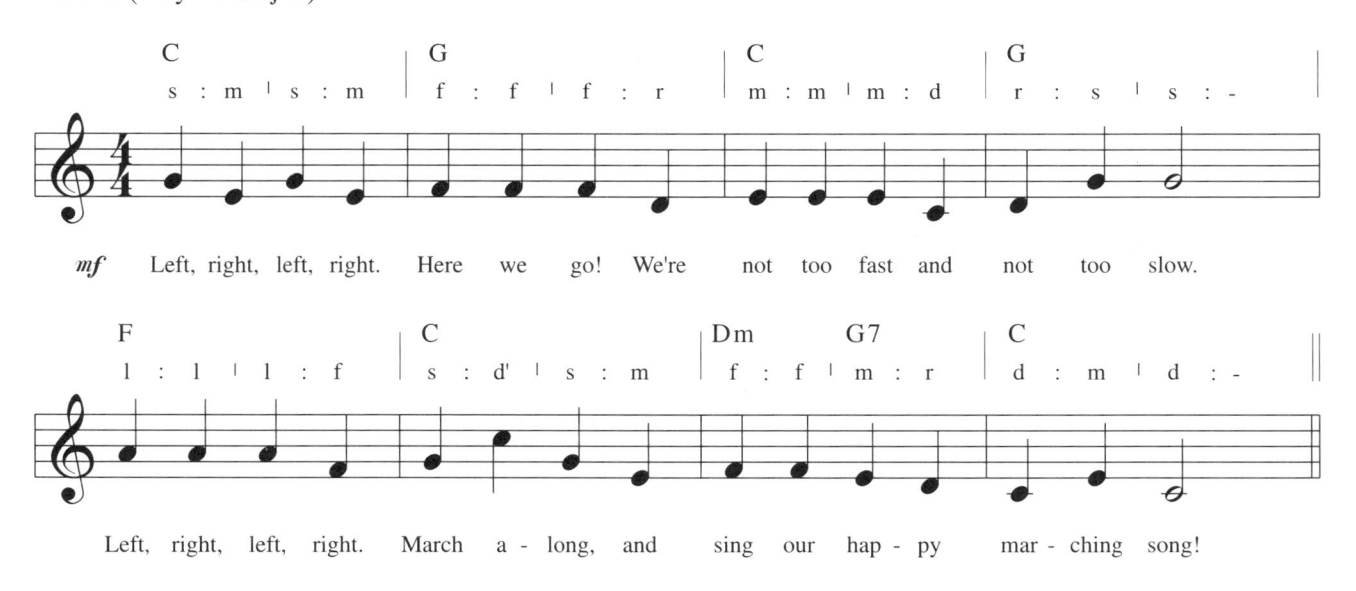

| C | G | C | G |
| s : m | s : m | f : f | f : r | m : m | m : d | r : s | s : - |

mf Left, right, left, right. Here we go! We're not too fast and not too slow.

| F | C | Dm | G7 | C |
| l : l | l : f | s : d' | s : m | f : f | m : r | d : m | d : - |

Left, right, left, right. March a-long, and sing our hap-py mar-ching song!

Jabulani's passengers may not have a smooth ride, but they do have fun bouncing up and down. Do have a ricksha ride when you visit Durban!

Jabulani, the ricksha man
(Zulu)

Jabulani
The ricksha man
Leaps in the air
As high as he can!

His passengers laugh
As they bounce inside.
'Isn't it fun
On a ricksha ride?'

'Hamba kahle, Jabulani!
Hamba kahle,' we all say.
'Sala kahle,' he replies
'Come again another day!'

Let's be . . . JABULANI

Place hand bells on wrists and/or ankles to jingle as Jabulani's do.

Divide the class into 'passengers' and 'Jabulani'.

Lines 7 and 8: All clap the rhythm.

Introduce the children to a variety of greetings in different languages to be used at the beginning and end of each day. Refer to the songs and poems in the first section, 'Greetings'.

Hamba kahle means 'Go well'; Sala kahle means 'Goodbye' in Zulu.

RUN ALONG

Lightly
Doh: D (Key: D major)

```
    D
    d . r : m . r | d . r : m . r | d . s : s . s | s : —
p   Lis-ten  to  the  run-ning  mu-sic    as   we  run  a-long.
                                                              mf

    G         D         Em        D         A7              D
    l . l : s . s | f . f : m . m | r . f : r . t,  | d : —
    It  goes run-ning, run-ning, run-ning,  to  this hap-py song!
```

The teacher plays the ♩ pulse on the hand drum while the children sing and clap the pattern and run around the room.

Kangaroo

She carries her baby
In her pouch
It's ever so comfy
He never cries 'ouch'.[1]
She can jump this high[2]
And leap so far[3]
The kangaroo from
Aus-tra-li-a! [4]

Sound effects

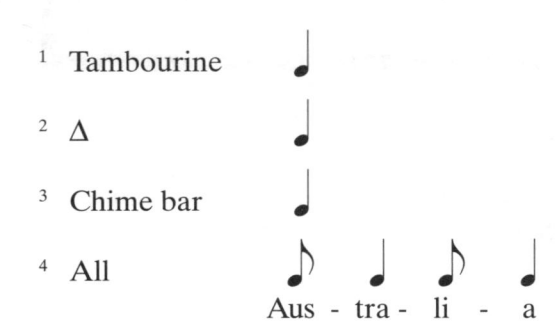

[1] Tambourine   ♩

[2] △   ♩

[3] Chime bar   ♩

[4] All   ♪ ♩ ♪ ♩
          Aus - tra - li - a

Let's be ... KANGAROOS

The children form a circle, with one child being the 'kangaroo' in the centre. All say the poem. The 'kangaroo' acts out the action.

EVERY WAY

A steady beat
Doh: C (Key: C major)

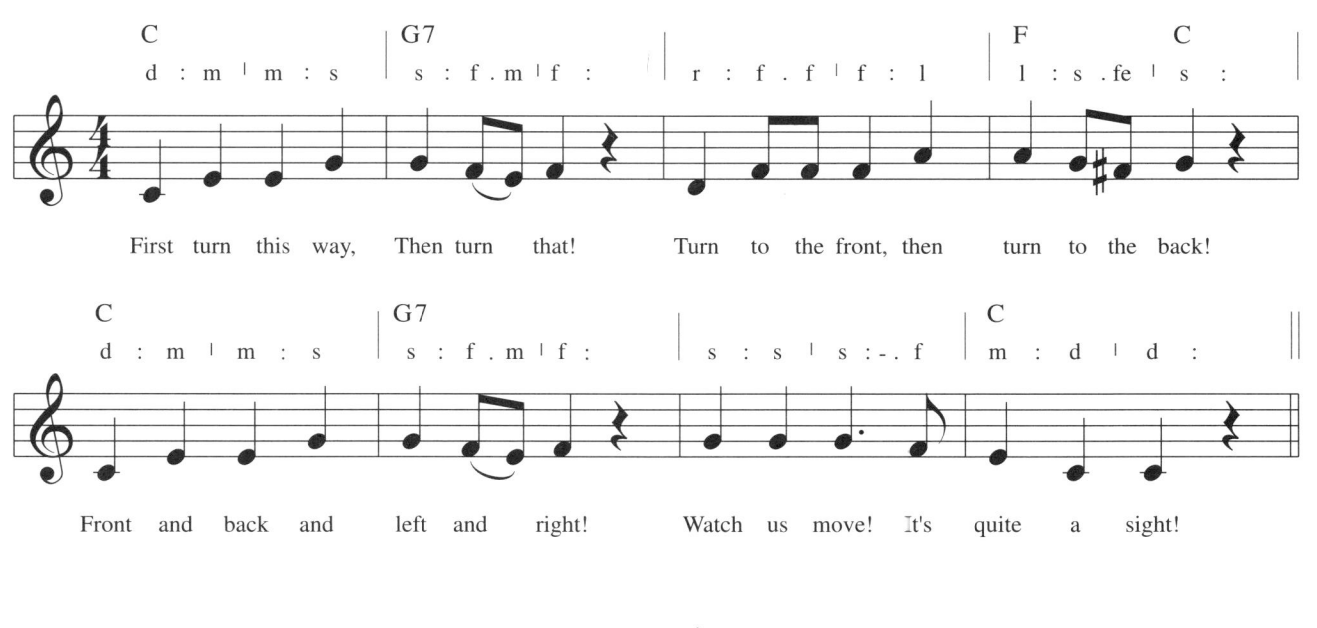

C	G7		F C
d :m | m : s	s : f.m | f :	r : f.f | f : l	l : s .fe | s :

First turn this way, Then turn that! Turn to the front, then turn to the back!

C	G7		C
d :m | m : s	s : f.m | f :	s : s | s :-. f	m : d | d :

Front and back and left and right! Watch us move! It's quite a sight!

Crabs

Crabs walk
From side to side,
In the rocks
They love to hide.

If WE walked
From side to side
I'm quite sure
We'd soon collide![1]

[1] The children make their own 'colliding sounds'.

> ### Let's be . . . CRABS
>
> The children walk quietly, step-together to the right, then to the left. All say the poem ending with one group choosing and making the 'colliding' sound effect.

WHAT'S IN A NAME?

The song-o-lo-lo and the mi-lli-pede are the same. The on-ly diff'-rence is the name.

Accompaniment

Divide the class into three groups.

Group A — Says the speech pattern.

Group B — 'The millipedes' pat their name
mi - lli - pede

Group C — 'The songololos' clap their name
song - o - lo - lo

Start the accompaniment at the first complete bar.
These may be done separately or together.

Let's be . . .
SONGOLOLOS (follow my leader)

The children form a line. The 'head' leads the way in free movement around the room, followed by the 'body'.

The 'head' plays a walking or running beat on the hand drum. The 'body' moves accordingly.

When the drum stops, the 'head' moves to the 'tail', giving the second child a turn to lead.

The children may say the poem and clap the pulse or rhythmic pattern while moving.

The teacher may play the triangle for the 'head' to change direction.

Tell the children that . . .

A songololo (sometimes also called a 'shongololo') is the African name for the millipede with a hard, shiny coat. The songololo rolls into a coil when it is touched. Some people believe that if songololos come into the house, it is going to rain.

A song with contrasting moods and dynamics.

IT'S NOT FAIR!

Doh: F (Key: D minor)

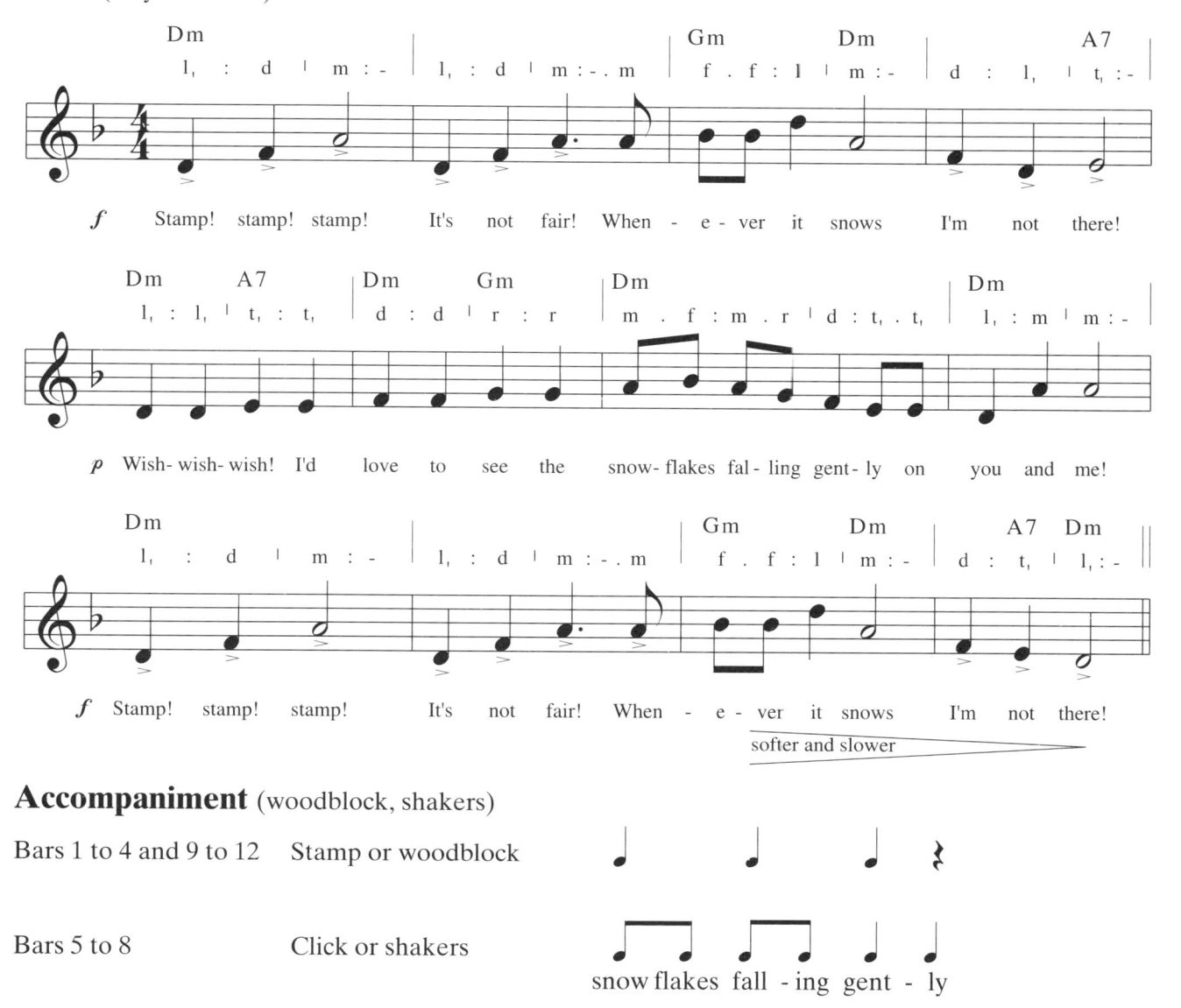

(Music notation with chords: Dm, Gm, Dm, A7, Dm, A7, Dm, Gm, Dm, Dm, Gm, Dm, A7 Dm)

f Stamp! stamp! stamp! It's not fair! When-e-ver it snows I'm not there!

p Wish-wish-wish! I'd love to see the snow-flakes fal-ling gent-ly on you and me!

f Stamp! stamp! stamp! It's not fair! When-e-ver it snows I'm not there!

softer and slower

Accompaniment (woodblock, shakers)

Bars 1 to 4 and 9 to 12   Stamp or woodblock   ♩ ♩ ♩ 𝄽

Bars 5 to 8   Click or shakers   ♫ ♫ ♩ ♩
                                                 snow flakes fall-ing gent-ly

---

Let's be ... THE CHILD AND THE SNOWFLAKES

Divide the class into three groups.

Group A   Sings the song.

Group B   Bars 1 to 4 stamp heavily.

Group C   Bars 5 to 8 tiptoe lightly on the spot.

🎓 *The children may choose shapes to identify the phrases and place shapes into the same order as the song is structured.*

DRUIWE

Doh: D (Key: D major)

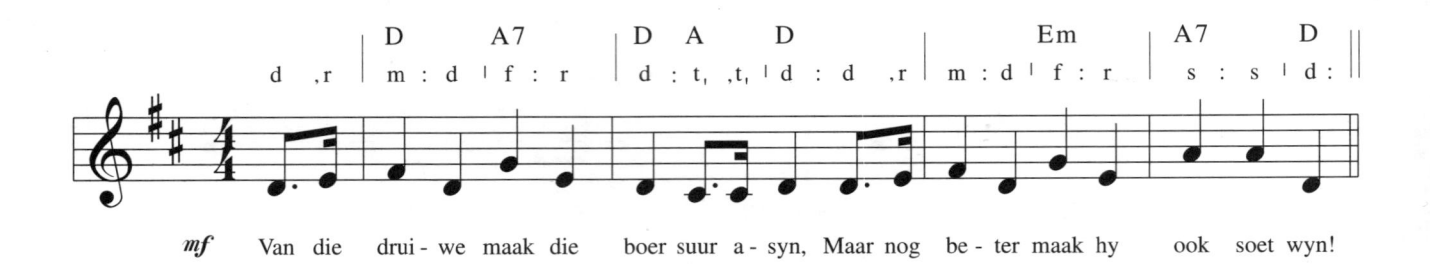

```
        | D      A7   | D    A    D    |              Em           | A7       D  |
      d ,r | m : d | f : r | d : t, ,t, | d : d ,r | m : d | f : r | s : s | d :
```

mf Van die drui-we maak die boer suur a-syn, Maar nog be-ter maak hy ook soet wyn!

Accompaniment (drum)

Play the ♩ pulse ♩ ♩ ♩ ♩ throughout.
                drui - we drui - we

> **Let's make . . . WINE**
> Stamp the ♩ pulse with feet 'on the spot', as the farmers do to the grapes.

Galloping

Let's gallop away
On Prince Hamlet my horse,
Clip-clop, clip-clop,
We're on the race-course!

Introduction, accompaniment and coda

Click ♪ ♩ ♪ ♩
      clip clop clip clop

SKIPPING HERE and SKIPPING THERE

Fairly fast and light
(Key: C major)

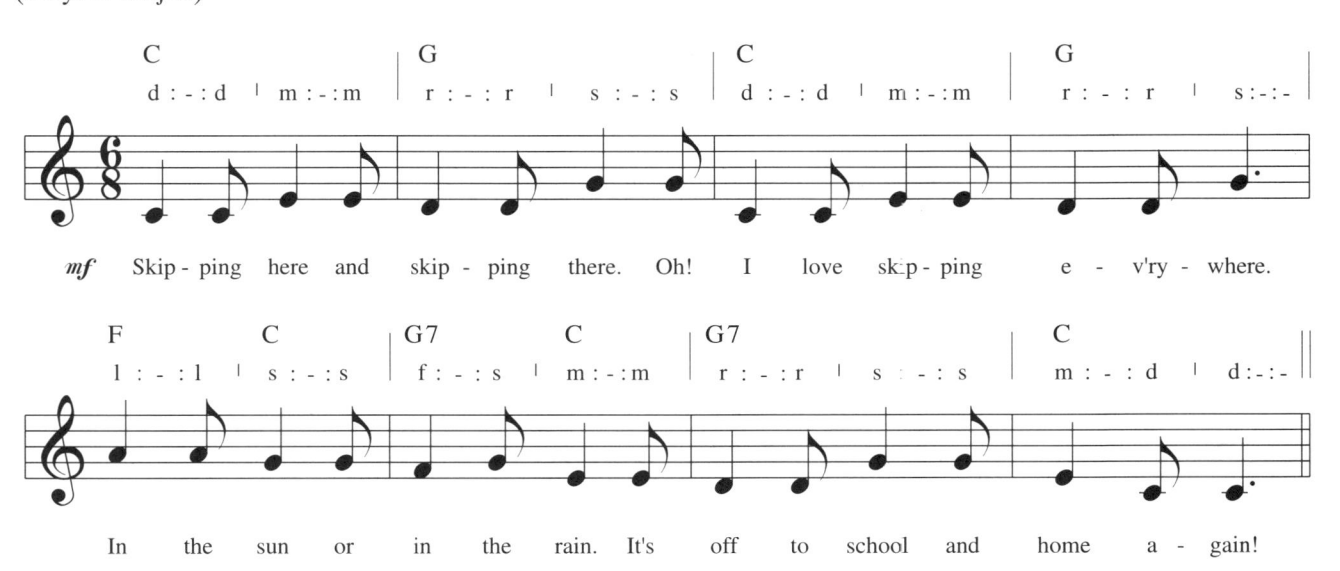

mf Skip-ping here and skip-ping there. Oh! I love skip-ping e-v'ry-where.
In the sun or in the rain. It's off to school and home a-gain!

Jumping beans

Thump! Thump! Bump!
Hear us[1] jump!

Just like a jumping bean,
The funniest sight you've EVER seen!

Thump! Thump! Bump!
Hear us jump!

[1] Use the children's names.

Let's be ... JUMPING BEANS

Let the fist jump on the floor. Then the tambourine beater may 'jump' (not too violently) on the tambourine. The children may jump heavily during lines 1, 2, 5 and 6 and jump lightly on-the-spot during lines 3 and 4.

Encourage the children to draw the different sections of the 'Jumping Beans' poem.

A change of speed.

TJOEK-TJOEK-TJOEK
(Afrikaans)

At a moderate speed
Doh: D (Key: D major)

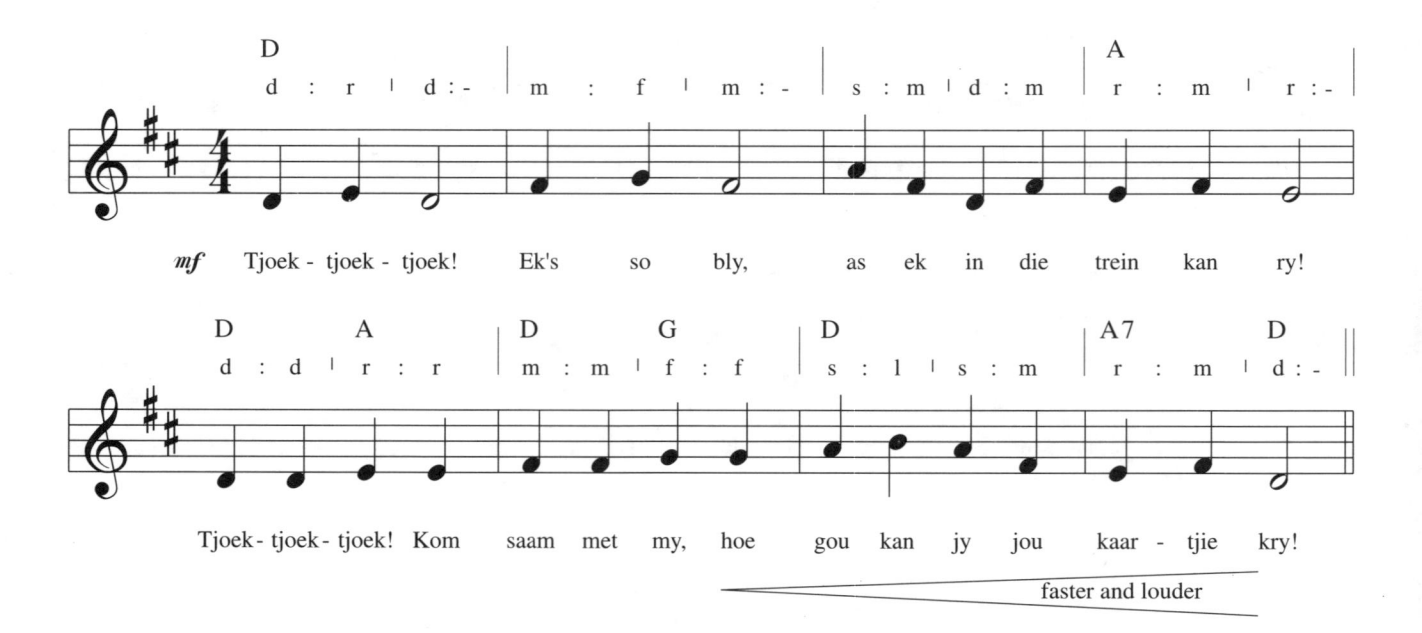

D				A
d : r	d :-	m : f	m :-	s : m	d : m	r : m	r :-

mf Tjoek - tjoek - tjoek! Ek's so bly, as ek in die trein kan ry!

D	A	D	G	D		A7	D
d : d	r : r	m : m	f : f	s : l	s : m	r : m	d :-	

Tjoek - tjoek - tjoek! Kom saam met my, hoe gou kan jy jou kaar - tjie kry!

faster and louder

Let's be . . . TRAINS

Encourage the children to make train sounds, whoo-oo-oo or tjoek-tjoek-tjoek, or the clicking of the wheels to introduce and conclude the song.

Mntwana uyajabula
(Zulu)

Umama beletha mntwana
Mntwana uyajabula!
Mntwana uyalala
Umama uyajabula!

The baby is happy
(Translated from Zulu)

The mother carries the baby on her back
The baby is happy.
The baby falls asleep,
The mother is happy!

Group A   Say and pat the pattern.

Group B   Click the ♩ pulse.

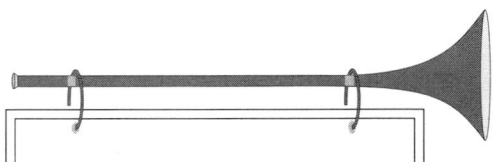

Tell the children that...

There are many words that mean 'mother'. In English we say mother, mommy, mummy, ma, mama. Encourage the children to tell you the word they use for 'mother'.

If I were a bee

Buzzzzz buzzzzz
If I were a bee
I'd make plenty of money
Selling for tea
My own brand of honey.

Buzzzzz buzzzzz
Pollen from here
Pollen from there
We'll arrive at the hive
Before you count five!

Buzz-buzz-buzz-buzz-buzz.

Let's be... BEES

Divide the class into two groups:

Group A   The 'flowers', who find their own space and remain there.

Group B   The 'bees' move among the flowers, stopping to take pollen with which to make honey.

The teacher plays five beats on a triangle and the bees 'fly' back to the 'hive'.

ASTRONAUT

Doh: C (Key: C major)

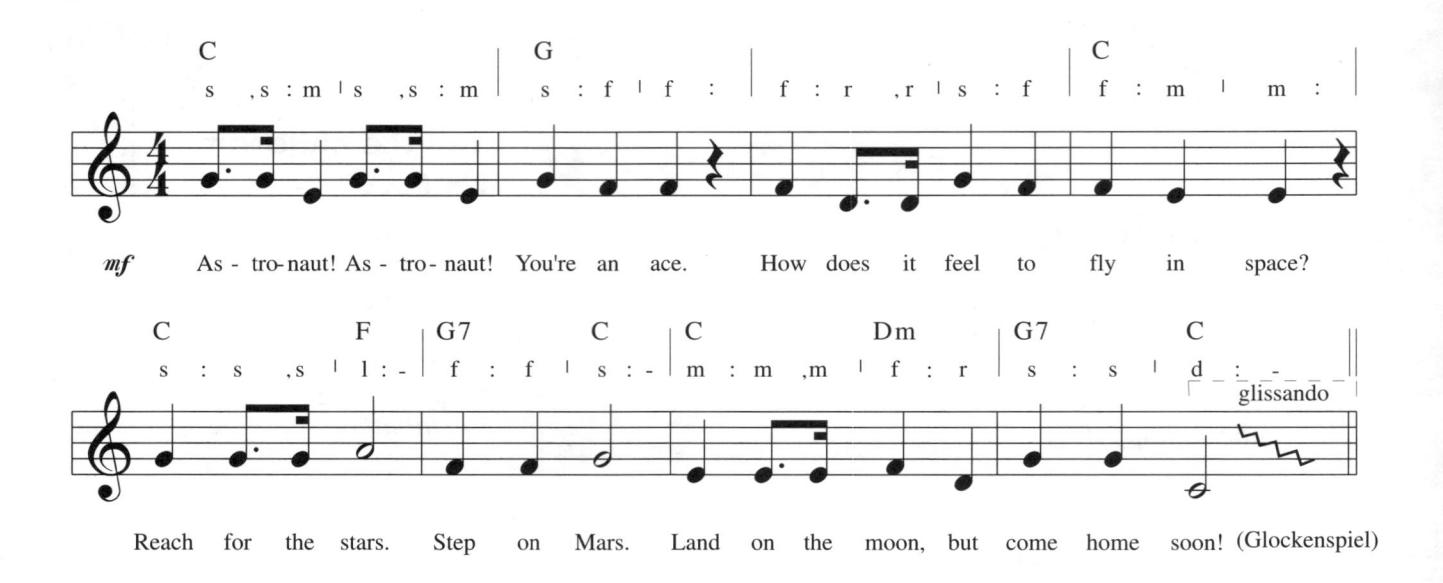

mf As-tro-naut! As-tro-naut! You're an ace. How does it feel to fly in space?
Reach for the stars. Step on Mars. Land on the moon, but come home soon! (Glockenspiel)

Accompaniment

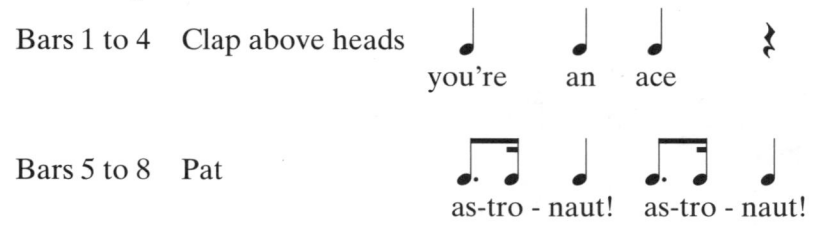

Bars 1 to 4   Clap above heads
you're an ace

Bars 5 to 8   Pat
as-tro-naut! as-tro-naut!

Let's be . . . ASTRONAUTS

Children move in a floppy, relaxed way as if floating in space.

Children may hum on one note or in ascending and/or descending patterns.

Glissandi or staccato notes on glockenspiel or chime bars may be played to accompany the song. The metallaphone with its resounding quality produces realistic 'space sounds'.

Glasses filled with water also make 'space sounds'. Play single notes rather than a glissando which could cause broken glass and flowing water!

A colourful poem.

Moths and butterflies

Moths are brown
They fly at night
Butterflies fly all day
Their wings are multi-coloured and bright
But they always fly away!

A poem with a message.

Drum beat

Can you hear the sound
Of the big, bass drum?

Themba¹ sends a message
With his hand and thumb.

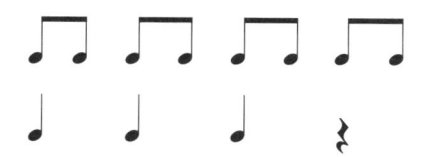

The rhythmic pattern of the verses is played on the drum.

¹ Substitute a child's name when it is his or her turn to clap the rhythm.

Encourage the children to create their own messages using body percussion or classroom instruments.

Umdanso wesic*athulo (Gumboot dance)

(Zulu)

Listen to the beat
Of the miners' feet
As they dance to the
Gumboot song.

Verse 2

The children create their own dance, stamping and clapping the rhythmic pattern of Verse 1.

Verse 3

It sounds so exciting
Like thunder and lightning
As they sing
And stamp along!

Verse 4

The children create their own instrumental verse, choosing instruments on which to play the pulse and rhythmic pattern of Verse 3.

Verse 5

Izic*athulo ziya danso danso	The shoes are dancing
Izic*athulo ziya le nale.	The shoes are going this way and that.

* click of tongue

Let's be . . . GUMBOOT DANCERS

The children improvise their own dance with body percussion, vocal sounds, instruments and movement. Wearing gumboots adds to the authenticity.

A horse may kick, as Vusi discovered.

UVusi ugibela ihashi *(Zulu)*   # Vusi rides a horse
(Translated from Zulu)

UVusi ugibela ihashi	drum	clip clop clip clop	Vusi rides a horse
Ihashi liyakhahlela	cymbals		The horse kicks
UVusi uyawa	xylophone	glissando	Vusi falls off
UVusi uyakhala!	triangle	tremolo	Vusi cries

ROBALA LESEA

(Tswana)

In a hushed whisper
Doh: C (Key: C major)

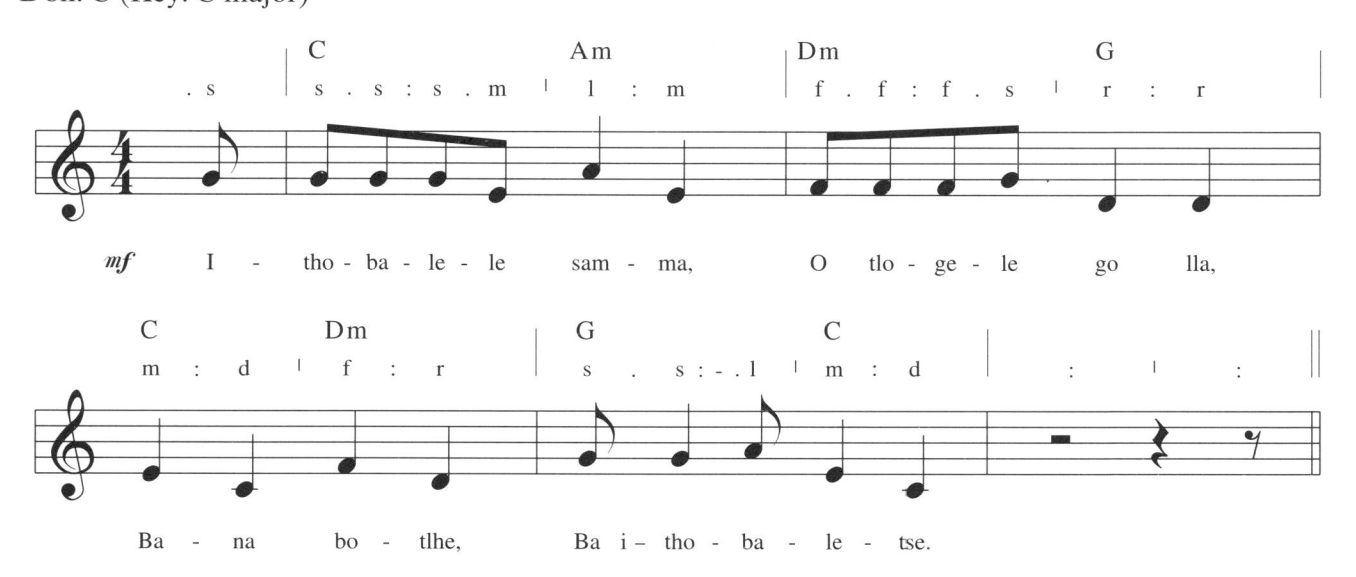

mf I - tho - ba - le - le sam - ma, O tlo - ge - le go lla,

Ba - na bo - tlhe, Ba i - tho - ba - le - tse.

Sleep, my baby

(Translated from Tswana)

Sleep my baby sleep
Forget about crying
All the babies
Are asleep.

Let's be . . . BABIES

Children rock gently to the ♩ pulse of the song.

Let's celebrate

Sunday is the Christian Day of Rest.

SUNDAY CHIMES

A happy song with a 'bouncy beat'
Doh: C (Key: C major)

C	F	G	C
s : m | s :-.s	l : f | l :-.t	t . t | l :-.t	d' : m' | d' :-

Ding dong ding! The church bells ring! Off we go to pray and sing!

C	F	G	C
s : m | s :-.s	l . l : f | l : l	t.t : t.t | l.l : t.t	d' : m' | d' :-

Lah - lah - lah! the or - gan sounds grand. All in - stru - ments to - ge - ther like a gi - ant band!

Accompaniment (xylophone, glockenspiel)

Xylophone   L R L R   L R L R
              Glockenspiel

Bars 3 and 4, 7 and 8 △ Tremolo

Tell the children that...

An organ has special 'stops' that the organist pulls out or presses to produce the sounds of other instruments. The modern electronic keyboard produces the sounds electronically.

Take the class to see and hear a church organ. They will be fascinated by its size and sound.

A band may be a group of people playing instruments together.

Welcome, Shabbat

From Sunday to Friday
We do our best
But Saturday is our
Day of rest!

Imma* bakes two challot
Plaited and light
For us to enjoy
On Friday night.

Don't forget the wine
And candles bright
To welcome Shabbat
On Friday night.

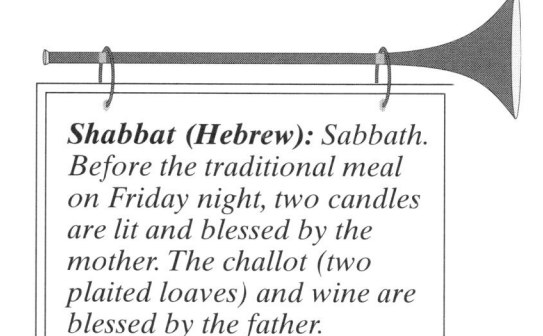

*Imma means 'mother' in Hebrew.

Shabbat (Hebrew): Sabbath. Before the traditional meal on Friday night, two candles are lit and blessed by the mother. The challot (two plaited loaves) and wine are blessed by the father.

Yusuf's way

From the minaret so tall
Yusuf hears the muezzin's call
To come and pray
In the mosque today.

Yusuf takes off his shoes
In a respectful way
Before he enters
The mosque each day.

Mosque (Muslim): A temple with a minaret, a tall turret, from which the muezzin, the crier, proclaims the hours of prayer.

Ramadan

Ramadan is the month
When Muslims fast
From sunrise to sunset
Until the month is past.

Nothing to eat,
Nothing to drink
Until the sun in the sky
Does sink.

Ramadan (Muslim): This is the month during which Muslims fast from sunrise to sunset.

Diwali (Deepavali)

Yatish loves
Diwali time!
Fireworks sparkle
And candles shine.

Whoosh! There's a red one!
Whoosh! There's a green!
The best fireworks
We've ever seen!

Sound effects

Line 4   ∆ Tremolo
Lines 5, 6   Shake shakers or clash cymbals.

Diwali (Deepavali) (Hindu): The Festival of Lights, this is the greatest Hindu Festival. It commemorates Rama's return to Ayodhya after destroying Ravana, the wicked king of Lanka. The people of Ayodhya were overjoyed and celebrated the return by lighting thousands of clay lamps. Today homes are decorated with rows of lamps. Sweets made of rice, thil (sesame seeds) and treacle are served.

Children enjoy the novelty of being asked to make a noise.

PURIM – A NOISY TIME

(Based on 'This Old Man', English traditional melody)

Doh: C (Key: C major)

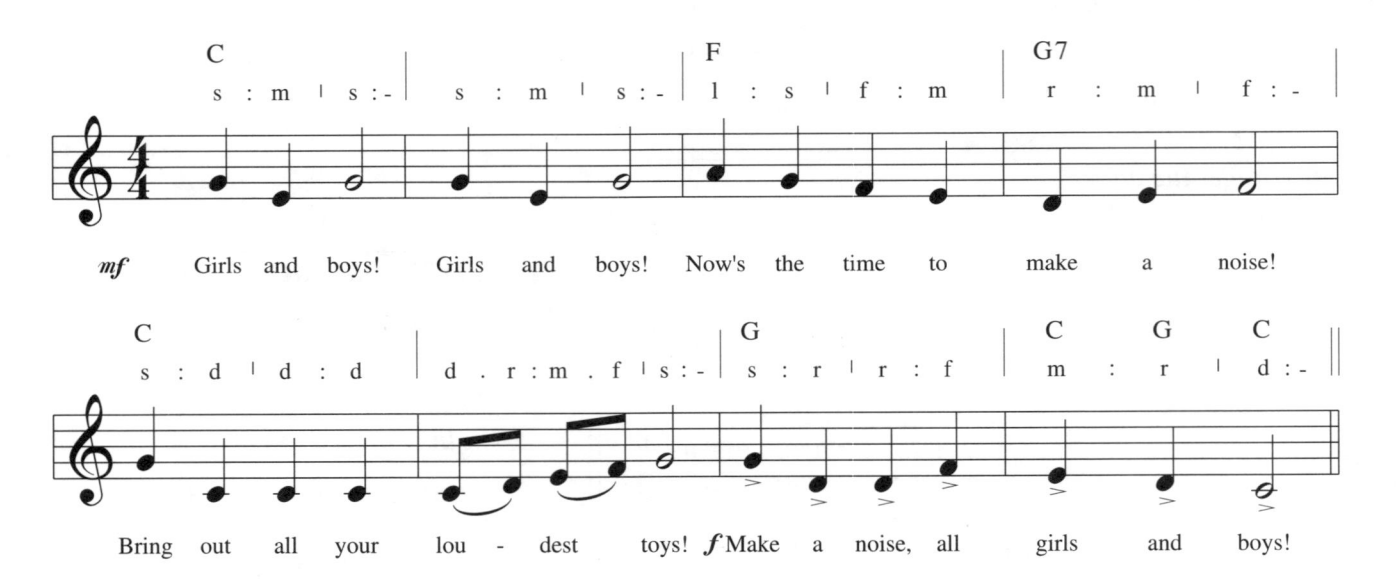

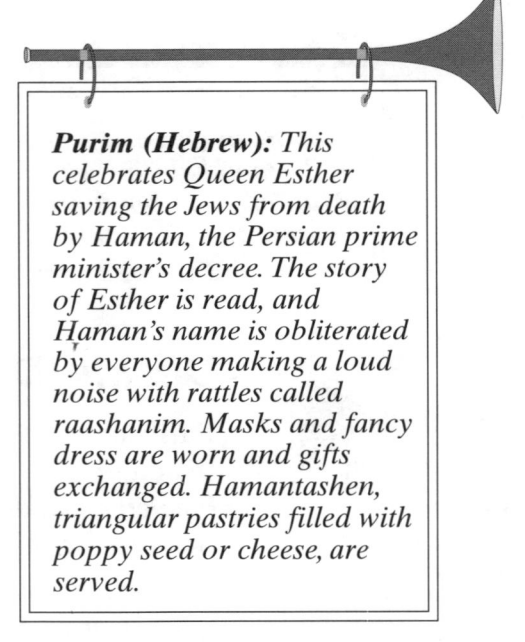

mf Girls and boys! Girls and boys! Now's the time to make a noise!
Bring out all your lou-dest toys! *f* Make a noise, all girls and boys!

Purim (Hebrew): *This celebrates Queen Esther saving the Jews from death by Haman, the Persian prime minister's decree. The story of Esther is read, and Haman's name is obliterated by everyone making a loud noise with rattles called raashanim. Masks and fancy dress are worn and gifts exchanged. Hamantashen, triangular pastries filled with poppy seed or cheese, are served.*

Accompaniment

Accompany the song with a body percussion accompaniment using a rhythmic pattern from the song.

Ask the children to listen carefully. How many times is ♩ ♩ ♩ heard? Encourage the children to try different ways of making the rhythmic pattern into a body percussion accompaniment.

HAMANTASHEN (Purim)

(Hebrew)

Doh: F (Key: F major)

Ha-man-ta-shen, Ha-man-ta-shen, filled with pop-py seed, We re-mem-ber Es-ther and her ve-ry brave deed! She saved the Jews from a ter-ri-ble fate. So e-vr'y Pu-rim we ce-le-brate. We eat

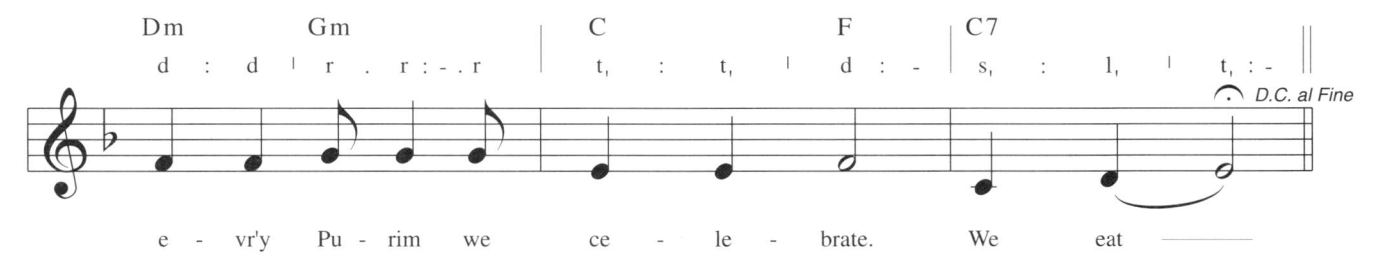

Accompaniment (tambourines)

Tambourines — brave deed

A song and dance to *Hamantashen*

Bars 1 to 4   Stand in circle. Hold hands. Run to the left.   A

Bars 3 to 8   Stand in circle. Clap   B

Bars 9 to 13   Take hands. Run to the right.   A

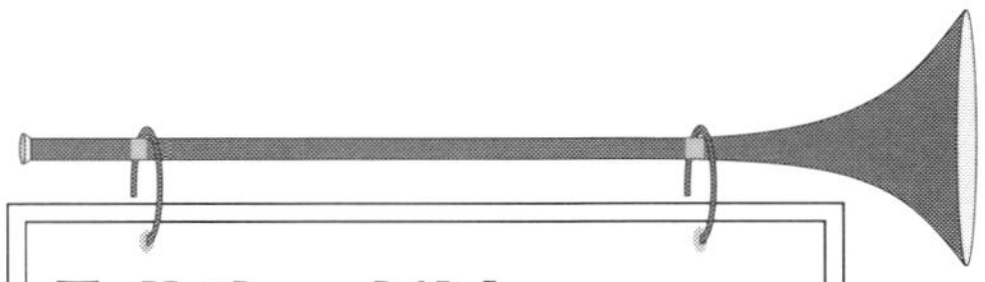

Tell the children that . . .

This song is like a hamantashen! A hamantashan is a triangular-shaped small pastry, with a poppy seed mixture inside a dough layer. The children paint and cut out △ shapes, some white, some white with black spots. These represent the dough and the poppyseed.

The children identify the repetition and contrast in the song.

△ △ △
A B A

Easter bunny

Easter bunny had to rush – rush – rush[1],
Painting eggs with his paint and brush.

Close your eyes – tight – tight – tight[2]
Will he leave one for me? He might – might – might![3]

Open your eyes as wide as can be –
I've found TWO eggs! Francois* has THREE!

Easter bunny is so kind!
If he painted eggs more often, I wouldn't mind!

*Substitute a child's name.

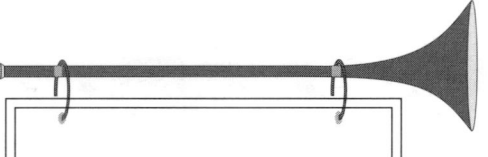

Easter (Christian): *This commemorates the crucifixion and rising from the dead of Christ. Hot cross buns, sweets and chocolates in the form of Easter eggs are eaten. The Easter bunny traditionally deposits Easter eggs for children to find and enjoy.*

Special effects and actions

[1] Flap wrists as if using a paintbrush.

[2] Clap hands or pat the floor ♩ ♩ ♩ at the repeated words.

Instrumental effects

[1] Shakers
[2] Tambourine
[3] Claves

Special days and ways

Whatever the language
Whatever the day
Everyone prays
In their own special way.

Invite friends of different cultures to visit the school to 'show and tell' about their religious festivals, music, art, dance and food. The children will enjoy talking about their 'special days and ways'.

A fun song to act.

HOT CROSS BUNS
(A traditional English song)

Doh: F (Key: F major)

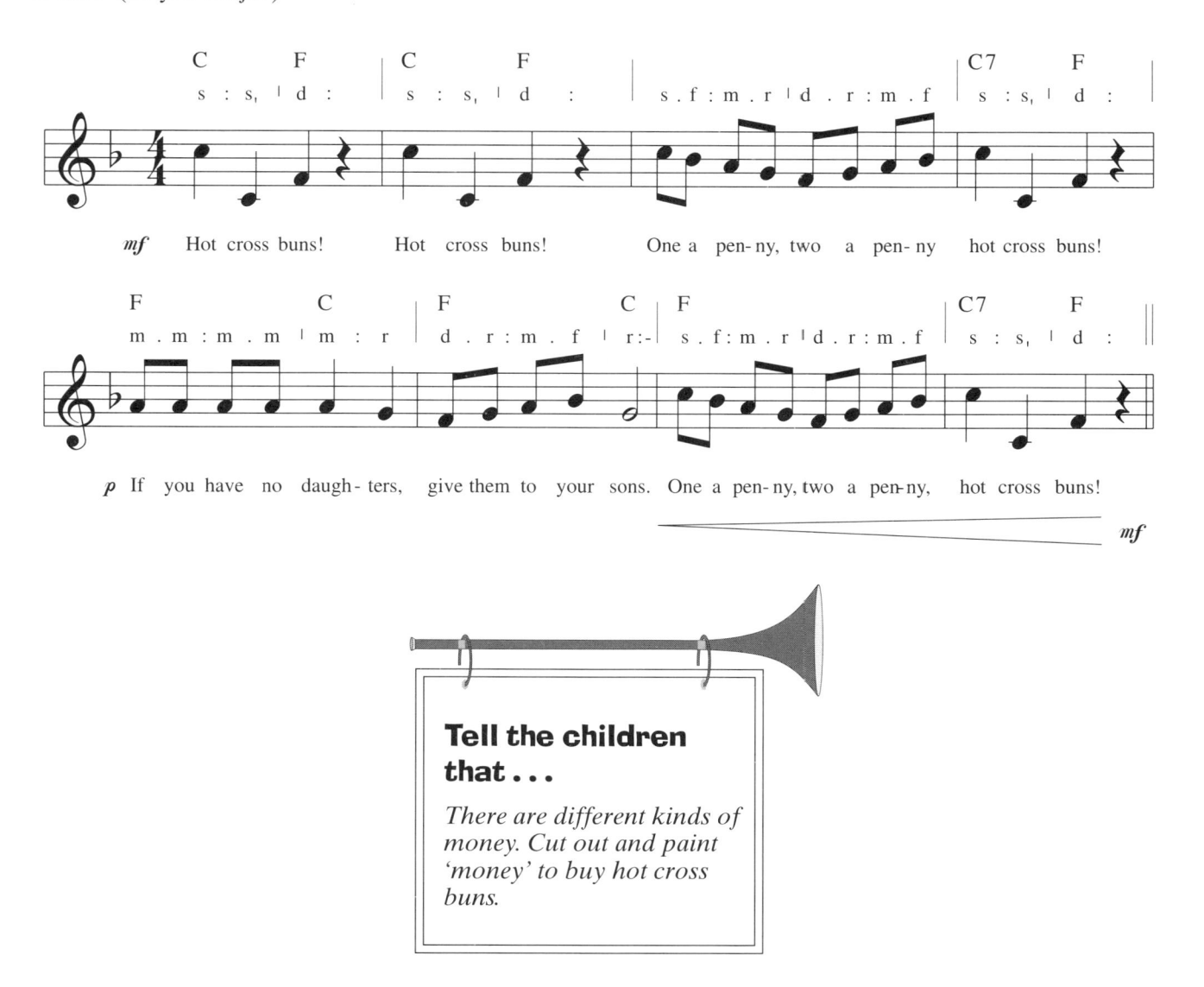

mf Hot cross buns! Hot cross buns! One a pen-ny, two a pen-ny hot cross buns!

p If you have no daugh-ters, give them to your sons. One a pen-ny, two a pen-ny, hot cross buns!

mf

Tell the children that...

There are different kinds of money. Cut out and paint 'money' to buy hot cross buns.

Show the children how the following two songs are based on this 'Hot Cross Buns' melody.

PAASBOLLETJIES
(Afrikaans)

Doh: F (Key: F major)

mf Paas-bol-le-tjies! Paas-bol-le-tjies! Gee my een of gee my twee. Paas-bol-le-tjies!

p Eet hul warm met bot-ter of ook met kon-fyt. Ma's in die kombuis, sy ja ons al-mal uit!
mf

PESACH-TIME

Doh: F (Key: F major)

mf Pe-sach time! Pe-sach time! Mat-za, chrain and soup with knei-dlach, Pe-sach time!

p Mo-ther's in the kit-chen, Bu-sy as can be! Pe-sach is the fa-v'rite time for our fam'-ly.
mf

Accompaniments for *Hot Cross Buns* songs

Body percussion accompaniment while song is softly hummed.

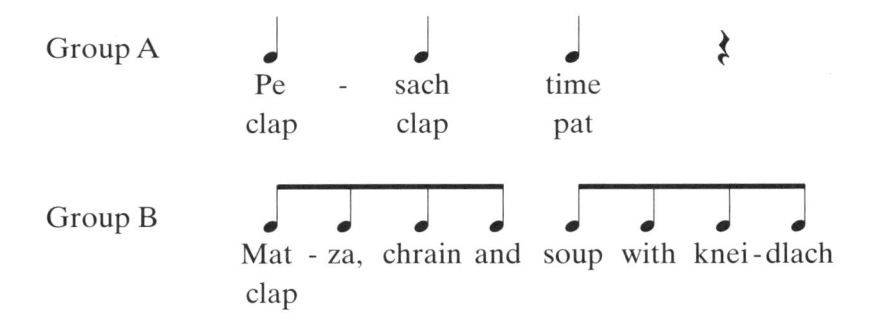

Group A

    Pe - sach   time
    clap clap   pat

Group B

    Mat - za, chrain and soup with knei-dlach
    clap

Pesach (Hebrew): *Passover. This commemorates the exodus from Egypt. Matza (unleavened bread), chrain (horse radish relish) and kneidlach (matza dumplings) are served. The story of the exodus is read during the meal.*

Instrumental accompaniments:

1. Tambourines   Pe - sach time   throughout.

2. Xylophone

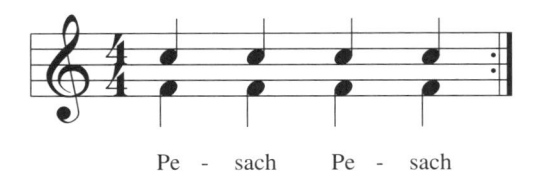

    Pe - sach Pe - sach

3. Chime bars or glockenspiel

    R L R

🎓 *Do not play the guitar chords when the children play the melodic accompaniments.*

A happy rhythmic song.

SHANA TOVA – Happy New Year

Doh: F (Key: D minor)

mp Sha - na to - va! Sha - na to - va! Sha - na to - va! Where -
e - ver you are! *mf* Hap - py New Year! Hap - py New Year!
Hap - py New Year! At last! Rosh Ha - sha - nah's here!

Rosh Hashanah (Hebrew):
New Year. 'Shana tova' is the greeting 'Have a happy New Year!' Apples dipped in honey are served to symbolize a sweet New Year.

Accompaniment

Bars 1 to 8   In pairs form a circle. Clap your own hands to the ♩ pulse.
Bars 9 to 16   Clap each other's hands together.

This song may continue into 'Apples and Honey' and return to 'Shana Tova', forming an ABA pattern.

Children can draw and cut out New Year cards and apples to represent the combined songs.

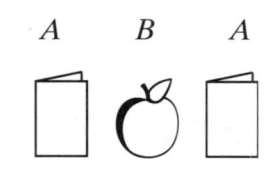

A B A

44

APPLES AND HONEY

With a lilt
Doh: F (Key: F major)

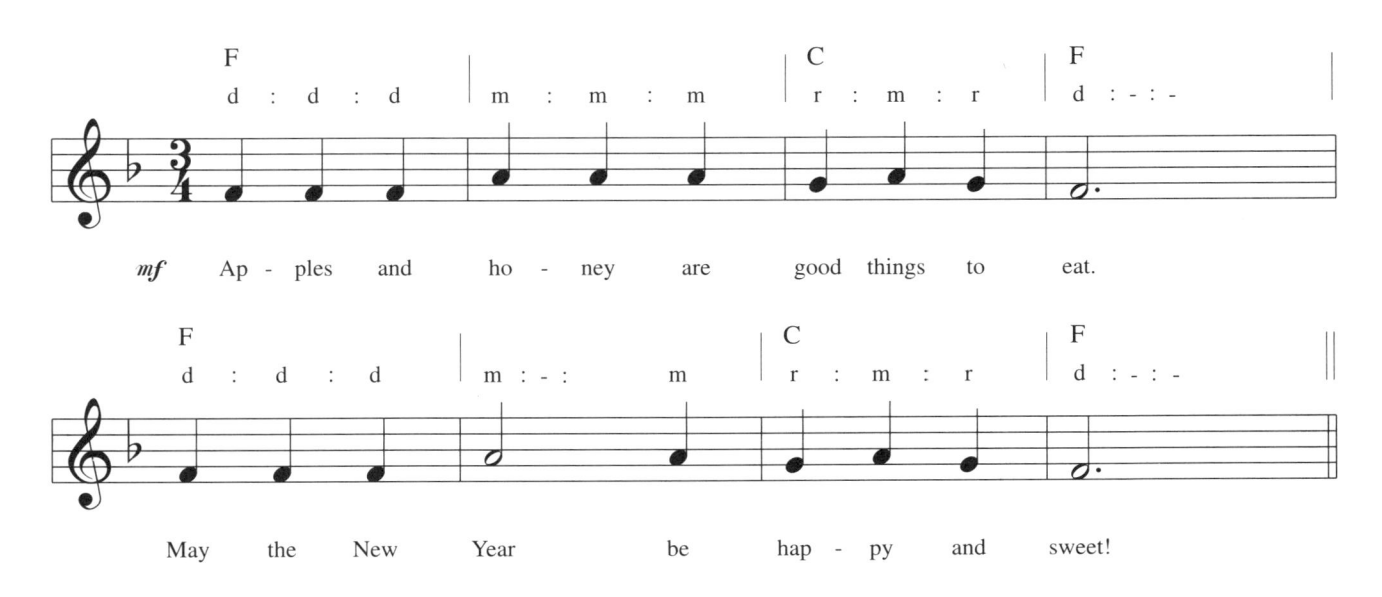

mf Ap - ples and ho - ney are good things to eat.

May the New Year be hap - py and sweet!

Accompaniment (chime bars)

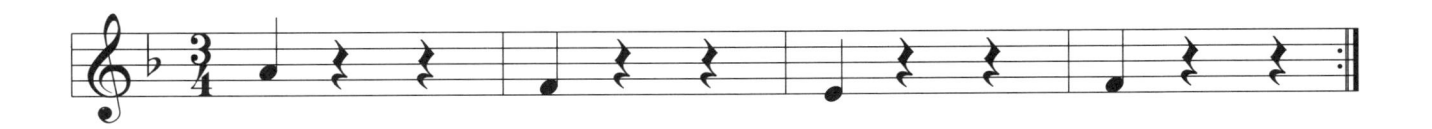

A song and dance for New Year

In a circle, stand, clap hands and sway

New / clap

Year / clap

45

A happy song.

SHAVUOT

Doh: F (Key: F major)

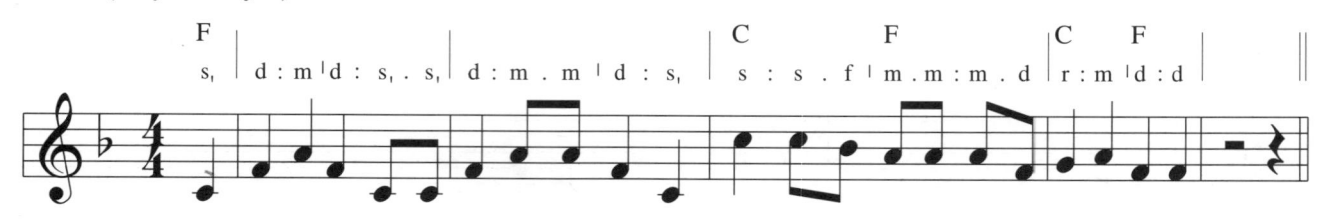

F			C	F	C	F
s,	d : m | d : s, . s,	d : m . m | d : s,	s : s . f | m . m : m . d	r : m | d : d

mf It's Sha-vu-ot, come as soon as you're a-ble, Blin-tzes with cin-na-mon are on the ta-ble!

Shavuot (Hebrew):
Festival of Weeks, or First Fruits. This commemorates Moses receiving the Ten Commandments on Mount Sinai, and the year's first harvest. Cheese blintzes (crepes) are served.

Accompaniment throughout (xylophone, chime bars)

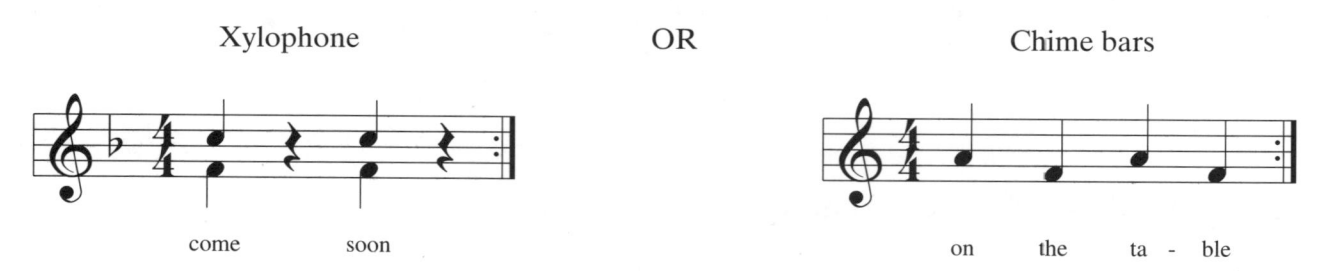

Xylophone OR Chime bars

come   soon   on the ta - ble

46

SUCCOTH IS HERE!

With a steady beat
Doh: D (Key: D major)

Lyrics: Suc-coth is here, ab-ba, im-ma, it's time to build our own suc-cah! With flo-wers and fruit for de-cor-a-tion, Succoth's the time for ce-le-bra-tion!

Accompaniment (tambourines)

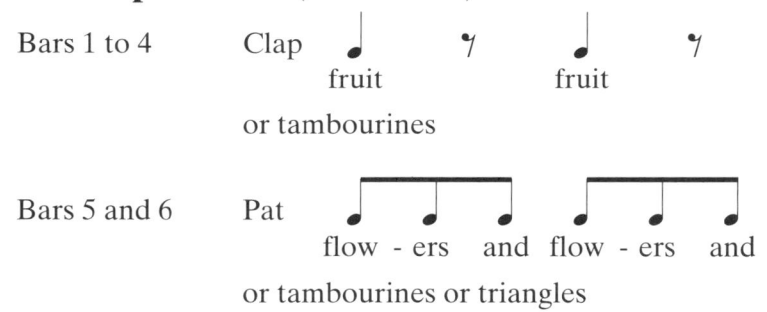

Bars 1 to 4   Clap   fruit   fruit
               or tambourines

Bars 5 and 6   Pat   flow-ers and flow-ers and
               or tambourines or triangles

🎓 *Abba means 'father' and imma means 'mother' in Hebrew.*

A song and dance for Succoth

The children form two parallel lines, holding their hands up to form an arch, the roof of the Succah. The first couple skip through the arch, then join the end of the arch, and the next couple follow until all have had a turn.

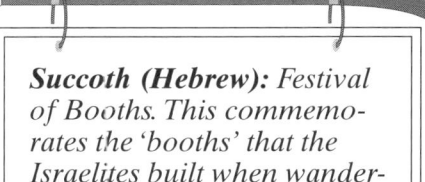

Succoth (Hebrew): *Festival of Booths. This commemorates the 'booths' that the Israelites built when wandering through the desert during the exodus. Families build their own 'succahs' and eat their meals there during the festival.*

A SPECIAL BIRTHDAY

Doh: C (Key: C major)

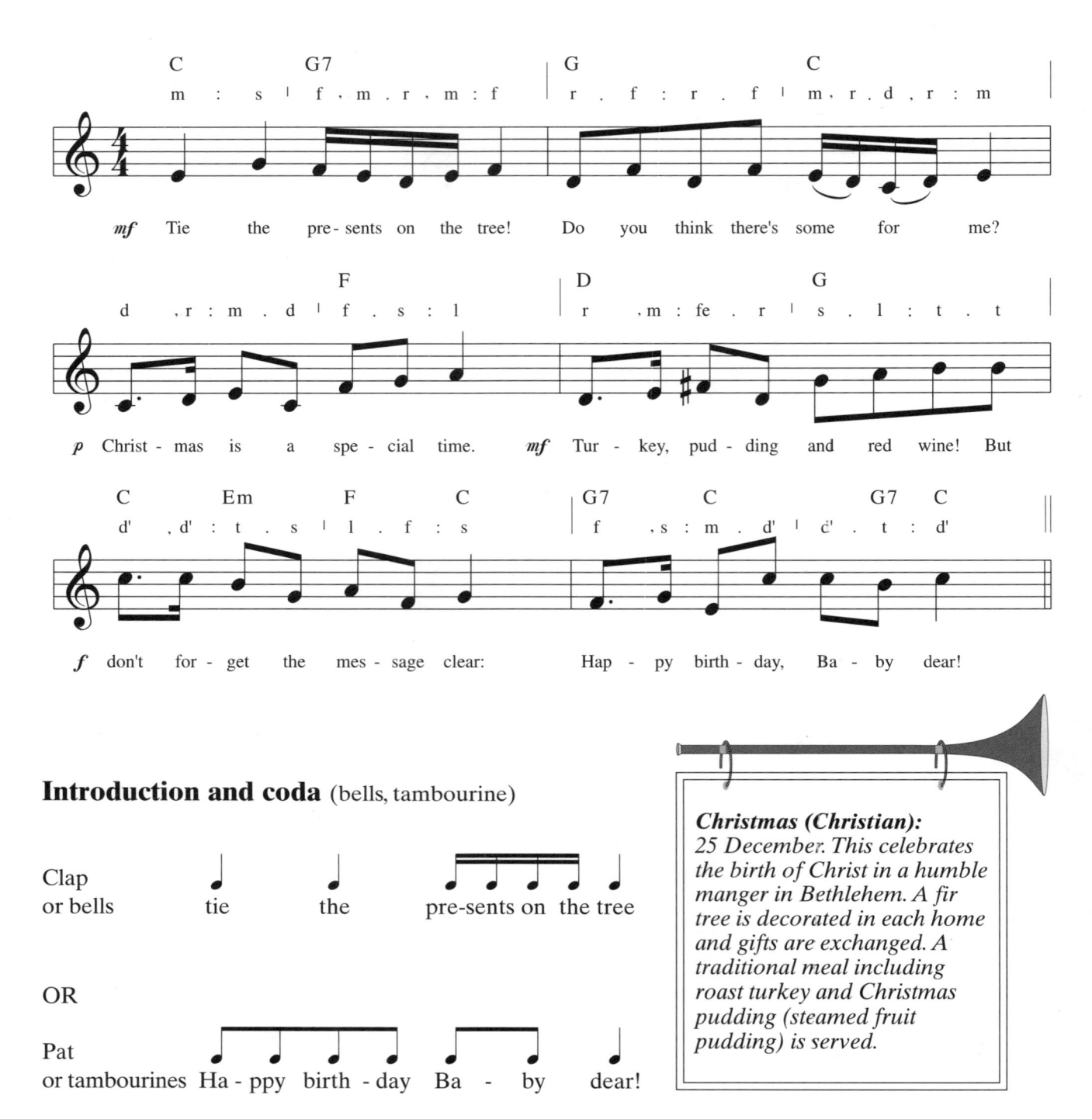

mf Tie the pre-sents on the tree! Do you think there's some for me?
p Christ-mas is a spe-cial time. *mf* Tur-key, pud-ding and red wine! But
f don't for-get the mes-sage clear: Hap-py birth-day, Ba-by dear!

Introduction and coda (bells, tambourine)

Clap or bells — tie the pre-sents on the tree

OR

Pat or tambourines — Ha-ppy birth-day Ba-by dear!

These patterns may be played separately or together.

Christmas (Christian):
25 December. This celebrates the birth of Christ in a humble manger in Bethlehem. A fir tree is decorated in each home and gifts are exchanged. A traditional meal including roast turkey and Christmas pudding (steamed fruit pudding) is served.

CHRISTMAS CAROL

Doh: (Key: D minor)

mf Long ago on a wintry night. People saw the strangest sight. A star shone in the sky so bright so we followed kings and shepherds that holy night.

Verse 2

No room at the inn so small,
Mary's babe was born in a stall
Sweet angel voices sang with joy
To welcome the darling little boy.

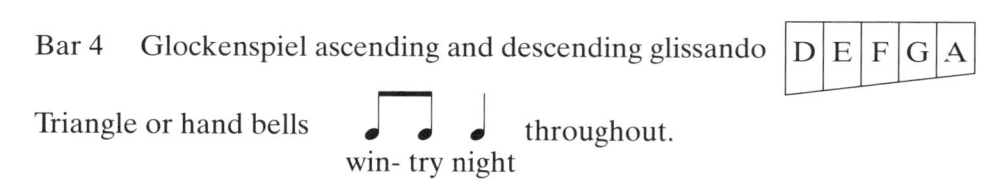

Accompaniment (glockenspiel, triangle, hand bells)

Bar 4   Glockenspiel ascending and descending glissando | D | E | F | G | A |

Triangle or hand bells ♪ ♪ ♩ throughout.
win- try night

CHANUKKAH

Doh: B♭ (Key: B♭ major)

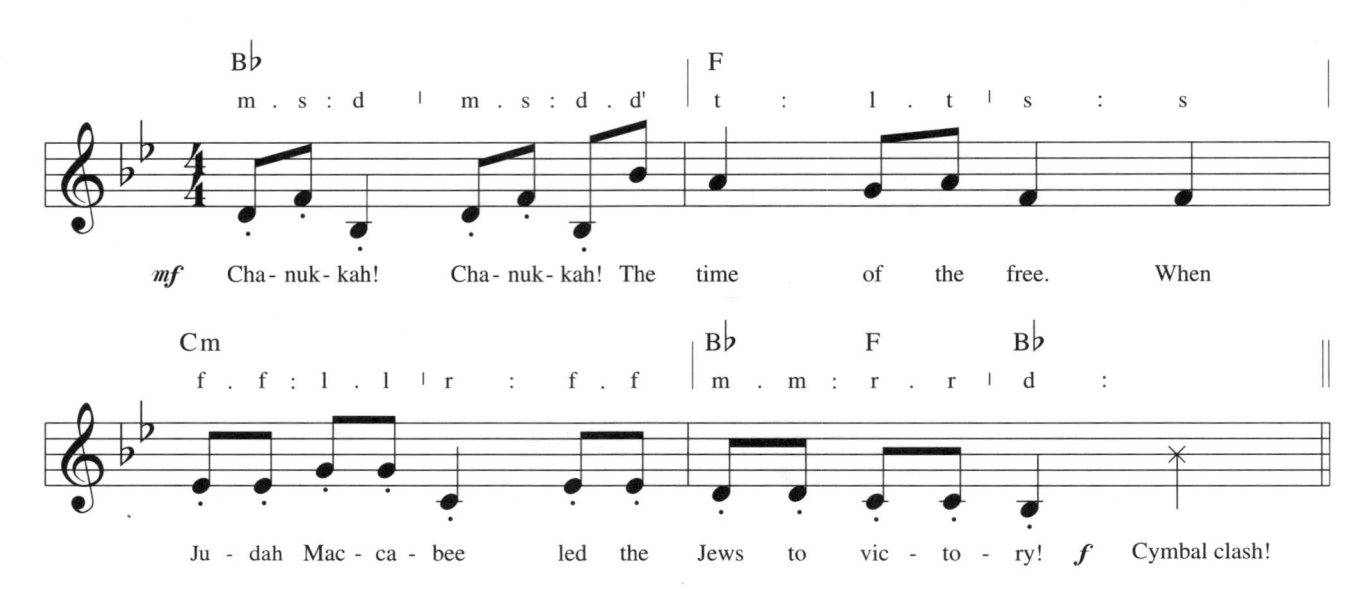

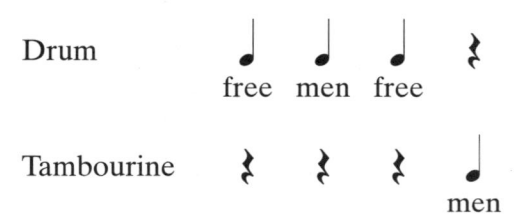

mf Cha-nuk-kah! Cha-nuk-kah! The time of the free. When Ju-dah Mac-ca-bee led the Jews to vic-to-ry! *f* Cymbal clash!

Accompaniment (drum, tambourine)

Drum: free men free

Tambourine: men

Chanukkah (Hebrew): *This celebrates the victory of the Jews, led by Judah Maccabee over the Syrians. Oil that was sufficient for only one night burnt miraculously for eight. The victory is commemorated by a 'menorah', an eight-candled candelabra. Children play with tops called dreidels. Potato latkes (fritters) are served and gifts exchanged.*

MY CHANUKKAH DREIDEL

(Traditional Russian folk tune)

A gentle swaying tune
Doh: G (Key: E minor)

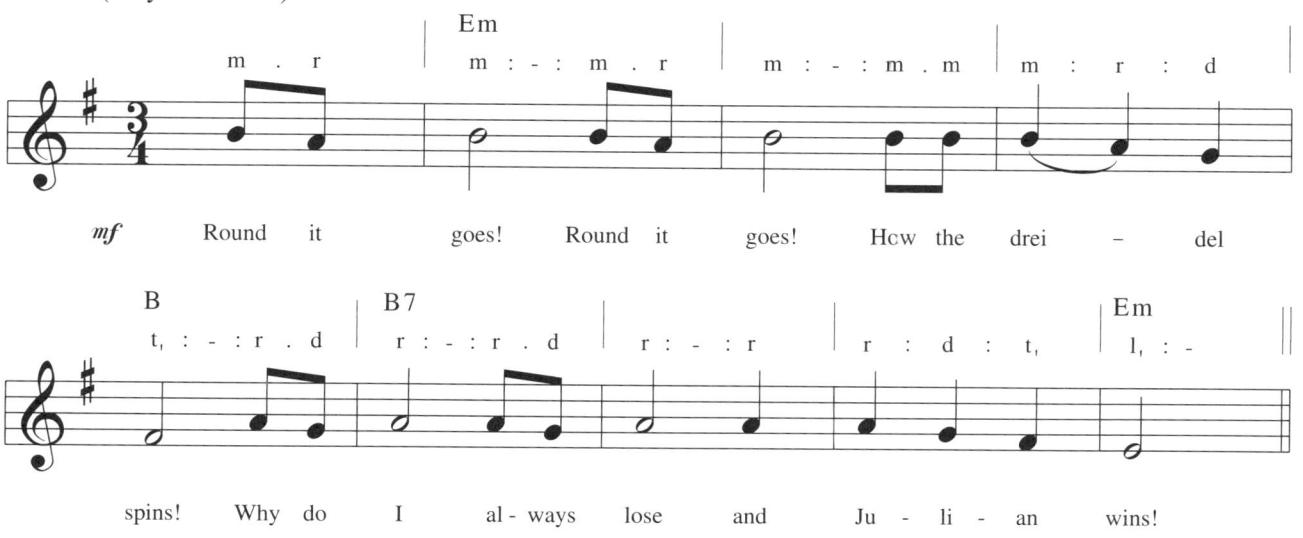

mf Round it goes! Round it goes! How the drei – del spins! Why do I al - ways lose and Ju - li - an wins!

Verse 2

Round it goes! Round it goes!
Will it never stop?
My whirring, turning
Chanukkah top!

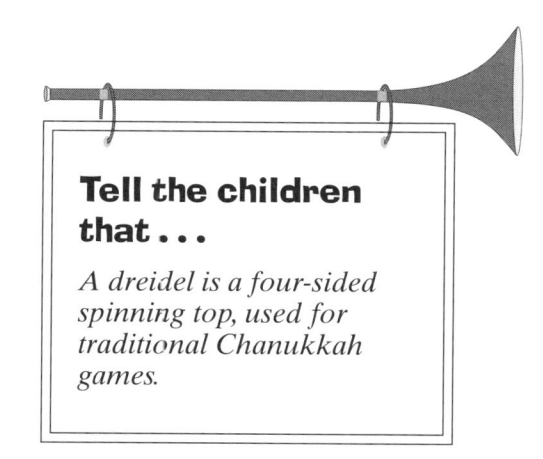

Tell the children that...

A dreidel is a four-sided spinning top, used for traditional Chanukkah games.

Let's be... DREIDELS

Children 'spin' round by jumping or by making tiny tip-toe steps in a small circle. Some will enjoy curling into a small ball and rolling from side to side, or they can sway gently from side to side as the dreidel moves slowly before stopping.

The seasons

Liyana! Liyana! (Zulu)

Liyana! Liyana!
Umlimi uyajabula!
Liyana! Liyana!

It's raining! It's raining! (Translated from Zulu)

It's raining! It's raining!
The farmer is happy!
It's raining! It's raining!

Sound effects

Clap ♪ ♪ ♪
      >
      Li - ya - na

Shake shakers and tambourines to make rain sounds throughout the poem. Pat the tambourines gently for a soft, rain effect.

A sad, lonely scene.

Winter se liedjie (Afrikaans)

Oostewind waai[1]
Groot, grys golwe
In die baai.[2]
Seemeeu skree[3]
'Winter is hier![4]
Winter is hier!'

Sound effects

Vocal

[1] oo – oo – oo
[2] sh – sh – sh
[3] ee – ee – ee (as in a seagull's screech)
[4] all together

AUTUMN LEAVES

At a leisurely speed
Doh: F (Key: D minor)

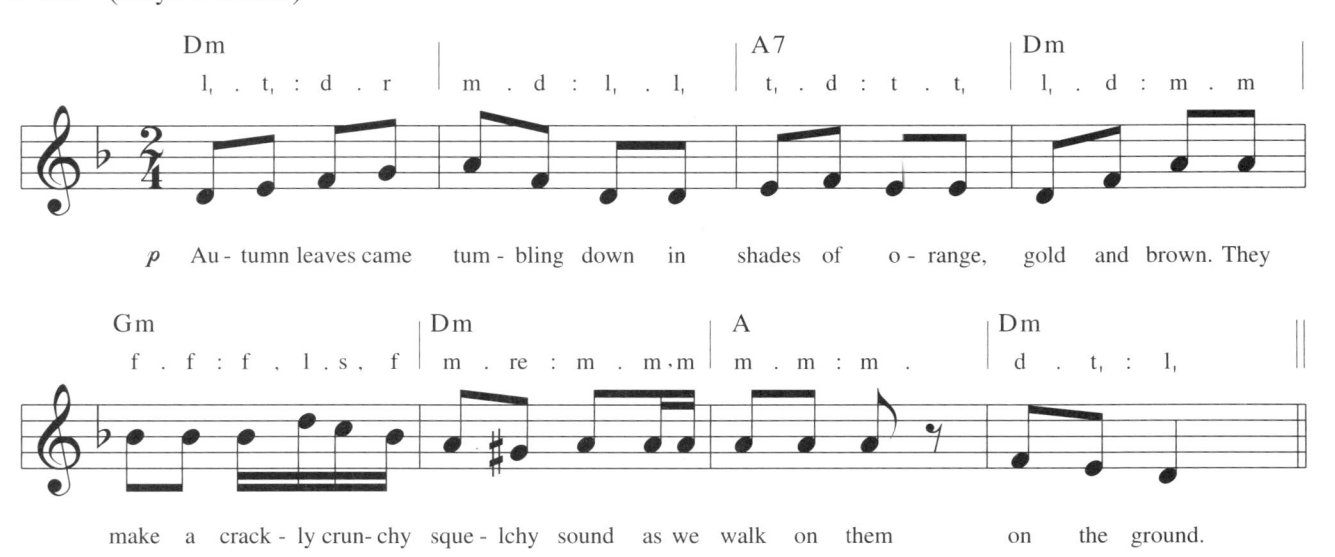

p Au-tumn leaves came tum-bling down in shades of o-range, gold and brown. They make a crack-ly crun-chy sque-lchy sound as we walk on them on the ground.

Speech pattern

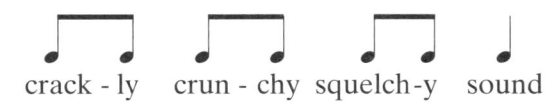

crack - ly crun - chy squelch - y sound

Pronounce the words slowly and clearly. Then say and clap the pattern throughout the song.

Accompaniment (bells, triangle and glockenspiel)

Bells and △ ♩ ♩ throughout the song.
walk walk

Bars 7 and 8   Glockenspiel, descending glissando.

Introduction and coda (glockenspiel)

Let's be . . . FALLING LEAVES

Move in a twirly way, like leaves being tossed by the wind.

Tell the children that . . .

They can draw the rise and fall of the melody line of 'Autumn Leaves'. It looks like leaves falling and being tossed around by the wind.

Draw a wavy line in autumn-coloured chalk or crayons. Encourage the children to make vocal sounds to interpret the melody line.

Granny and the weather

My granny is very particular
Wherever we go, near or far
'Take an umbrella, dear,
It might rain,
And a jersey,
It's chilly again.

'And don't forget your woolly hat
You'll catch cold if you don't take that!
Be careful!
'Cos that mild little breeze
Might get stronger
Then you'll sneeze! Atchoo!'

Dikgakologo (Tswana)

Dipula di a na[1]
Naga e tala
Dinonyane di a opela.[2]
Dipula di a na.[1]

Spring (Translated from Tswana)

It is raining
The land is green
The birds are singing.
It is raining.

Special effects (glockenspiel)

[1] Random descending notes to depict rain falling.

[2] G E G E   or sing bird calls.

YIVA INDUDUMA!

(Xhosa)

Happy and rhythmic
Doh: F (Key: F major)

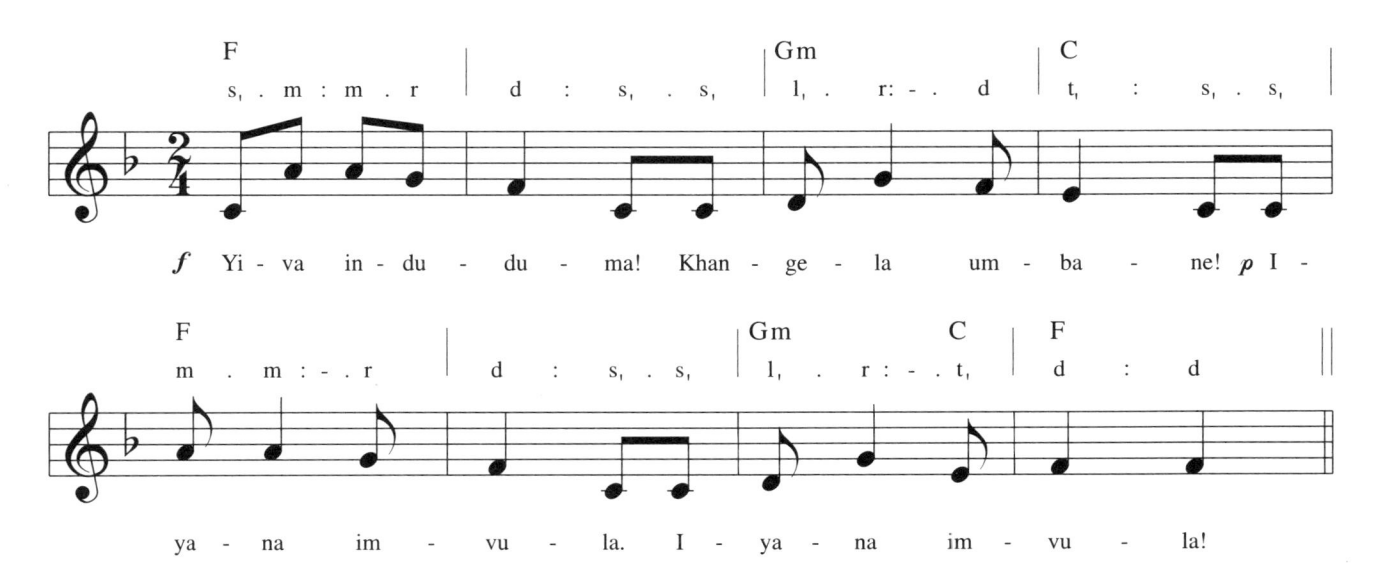

[Musical notation with lyrics:]
f Yi - va in - du - du - ma! Khan - ge - la um - ba - ne! *p* I -
ya - na im - vu - la. I - ya - na im - vu - la!

Hear the thunder! *(Translated from Xhosa)*

Hear the thunder!
Look at the lightning.
The rain is falling
The rain is falling.

Sound effects (drum, triangle)

Drum ostinato: children choose a rhythmic pattern from the song and play it throughout.

e.g. rain is fall - ing   or   im - vu - la

Bars 5 to 8   Triangle tremolo.

Whatever the weather

We have lots of fun at school,
Whether it's hot or whether it's cool!
Whatever the weather, I'm happy to say
We[1] love every single day!

[1] Substitute a child's name: Thuli loves . . .

The last line may be emphasised by adding body or instrumental percussion.

57

SOMER IS DIE BESTE TYD

(Afrikaans)

Doh: C (Key: C major)

C		F	C
d : - : r | m : - : r	d : - : s | s : - : -	l : - : s | f : - : l	s : - : m | s : - : -

mf So - mer is die bes - te tyd. Son en strand en vro - lik - heid.

F	C	F	G7	C
f : - : l | s : - : f	m : - : s | d' : - : -	f : - : f | m : - : r	m : - : d | d : - : -

p Win - ter is tog al te koud! *mf* Maak die vuur en kap nog hout!

Introduction and coda (xylophone)

Maak die vuur en kap nog hout!
R R L L L R R

Accompaniment (cymbal)

Bars 7 and 8 ♩ 𝄾 ♩ 𝄾
              kap   hout

HERFS
(Afrikaans)

A gentle, swaying song
Doh: D (Key: D major)

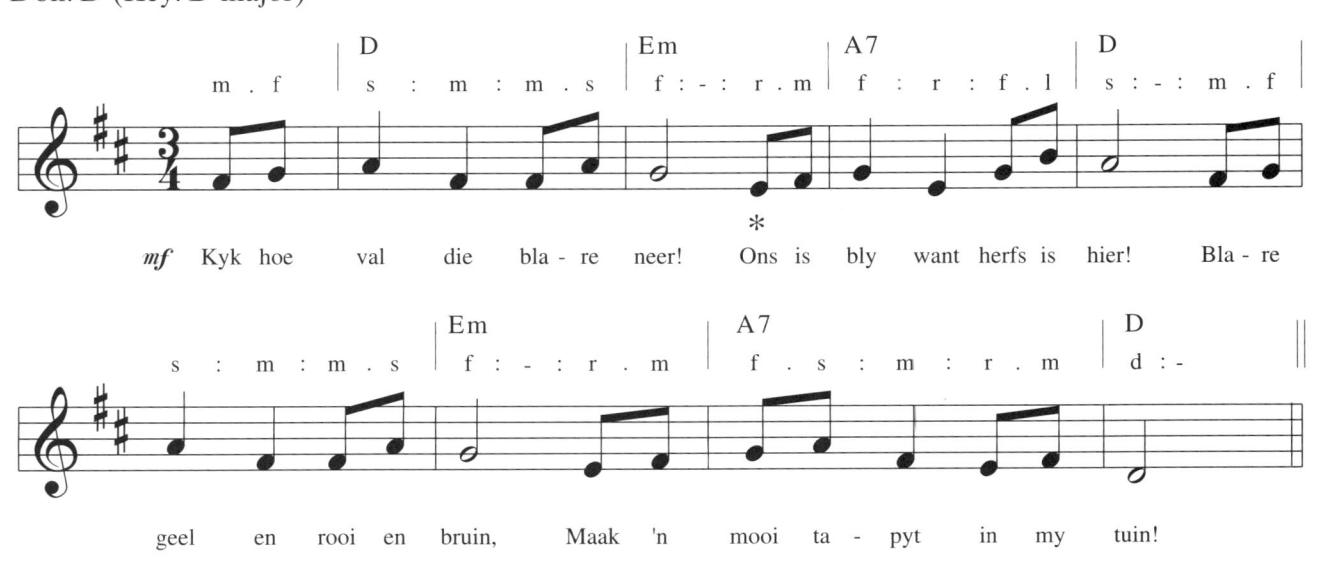

mf Kyk hoe val die bla-re neer! Ons is bly want herfs is hier!* Bla-re geel en rooi en bruin, Maak 'n mooi ta-pyt in my tuin!

*Substitute a child's name.

Accompaniment (xylophone)

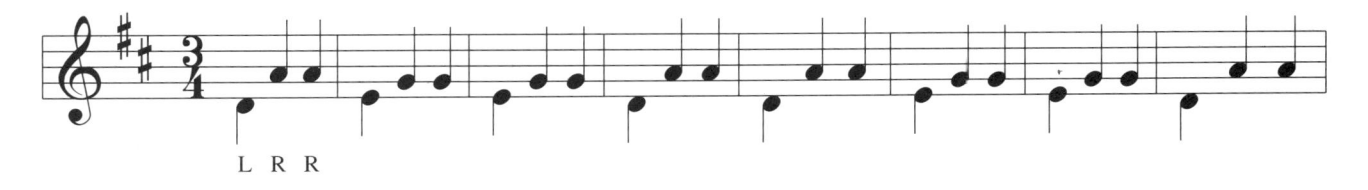

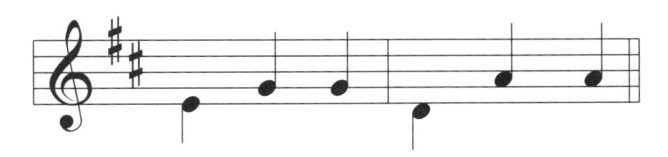

L R R

SPRING

A happy song
Doh: G (Key: G major)

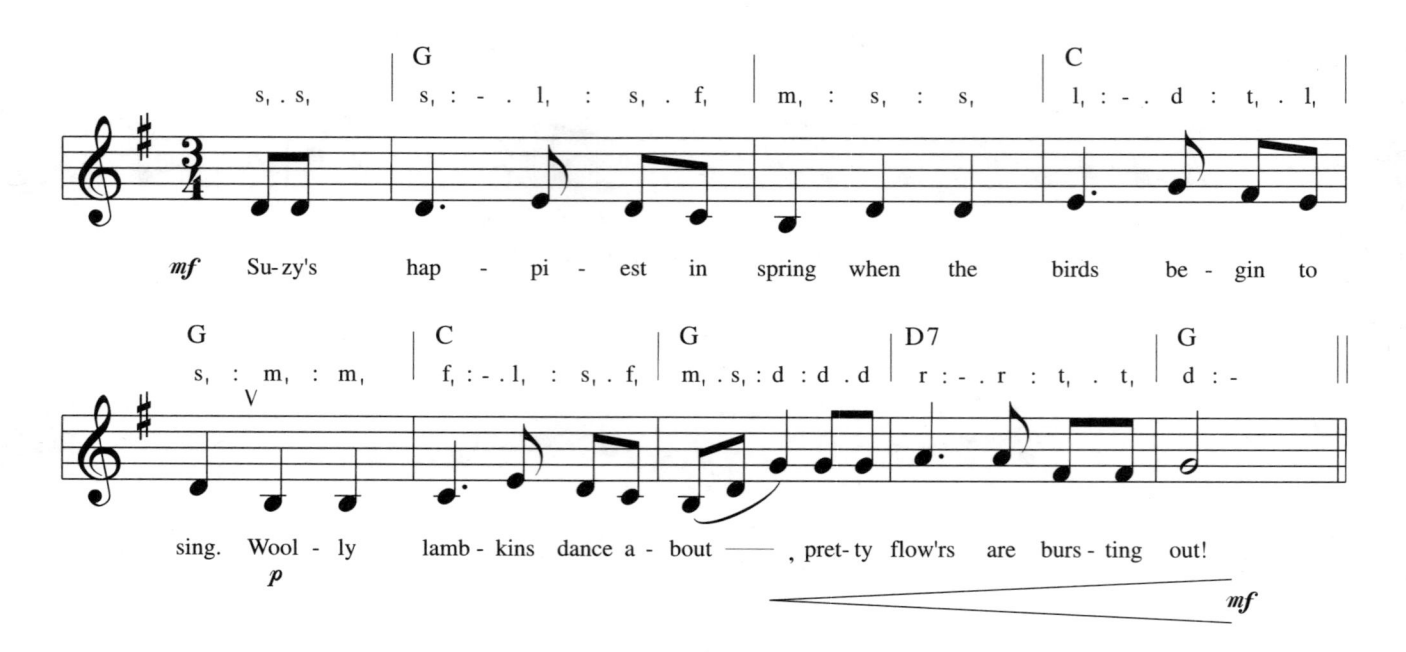

G		C	
s₁ . s₁	s₁ : — . l₁ : s₁ . f₁	m₁ : s₁ : s₁	l₁ : — . d : t₁ . l₁

mf Su-zy's hap - pi - est in spring when the birds be - gin to

G	C	G	D7	G
s₁ : m₁ : m₁	f₁ : — . l₁ : s₁ . f₁	m₁ . s₁ : d : d . d	r : — . r : t₁ . t₁	d : —

sing. Wool - ly lamb - kins dance a - bout ——, pret - ty flow'rs are burs - ting out!
p   *mf*

Accompaniment (tambourine, hand bells, triangle)

Tambourine   ♩ 𝄽 𝄽
             spring

Hand bells   𝄽 ♩ ♩
                birds sing

Bars 3 to 4   Triangle tremolo at 'birds begin to sing'.

ILANGA LIYASHONA

(Zulu)

Doh: C (Key: C major)

The sun is setting (Translated from Zulu)

Be quiet, be quiet my baby
Go to sleep,
The sun is setting
Be quiet, be quiet.

🎓 Divide the class into three groups.
  Group A   Sing the song.
  Group B   Sit and sway to melody A (Bars 1-4).
  Group C   Stand and clap the rhythmic pattern softly to melody B (Bars 5-8).
  Group B   Repeat their activity to melody A (Bars 9-12).

Encourage the children to use shapes or pictures or coloured paper to represent the sections.

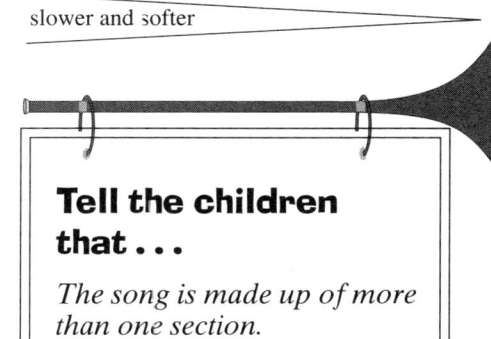

Tell the children that . . .

The song is made up of more than one section.
Sing the song for the children.
Let them hear and identify repeated and new melodies.

A happy holiday rhythmic pattern.

IHLOBO LISHUSHU!
(Xhosa)

I - hlo - bo li - shu - shu! Yi - za si - da - de! Yi - za si - dla - le! I - hlo - bo li - shu - shu!

Summer is hot! *(Translated from Xhosa)*

Summer is hot!
Let us swim
Let us play
Summer is hot!

Open your mouth wide to pronounce the words clearly. The children will then imitate you.

Divide the class into three, each group saying one phrase.

Group A: Phrase 1
Group B: Phrase 2
Group C: Phrase 3
Group A: Phrase 1

Encourage the children to create their own body percussion accompaniment to the pattern.

People and places

FLOWER SELLER'S SONG

Doh: C (Key: C major)

```
       C                          |G          C              |                   |  C
  s . s : s . f | m : d . d | r . r : t, . t, | d : d | s . s : s . f | m : d
```

mf "See my pret-ty flo-wers," the flo-wer sel-lers cry. "In bun-ches or in bas - kets

```
       F                          |C                          |G7         C
  l . l : l . s | f : d | s . s : s . f | m : d | r : s . d : -
```

at the pave - ment mar - kets, See my pret-ty flow - ers, won't you buy?"

p ———————————— *mf*

Verse 2

'See my pretty flowers,' the flower sellers cry.
'Strelitzia and daisies, gladioli, vygies,
See my pretty flowers, won't you buy?'

Verse 3

Encourage children to suggest other flowers. They need not rhyme.

Introduction, accompaniment and coda (1)

In pairs, children clap

Won't you buy?
clap   clap   clap-together

Introduction and coda (2)

Xylophone (bar 8)

won't you buy?

🎓 *The melody of bar 1 occurs more than once. Sing the song for the children. They raise their hands when they hear the bar 1 melody again (bars 1, 3 and 5).*

Table Mountain

See the tablecloth
Covering Table Mountain –
Van Hunks is smoking
His pipe like a fountain!

Tafelberg (Afrikaans)

Kyk na die wolke
Oor Tafelberg –
Dis Van Hunks se spook
Wat daarbo rook!

Tell the children that...

There is an old story about a Dutchman, Van Hunks, who smoked a pipe in competition with 'the devil'. When the cloud covers Table Mountain, people say 'Van Hunks is smoking his pipe again'!

All mountains do not have peaks. The top of Table Mountain looks as flat as a table-top. The huge cloud is called the 'tablecloth' because it looks like a tablecloth on top of the table. There is also a Table Mountain between Durban and Pietermaritzburg.

Children will enjoy making mountains with peaks and with flat tops from play-dough, adding a cotton wool tablecloth.

Pietermaritzburg

Pietermaritzburg
Is a capital city
With buildings old and new
And flowers, so pretty

Azaleas, red
Pink and white,
'Maritzburg in spring
Is a colourful sight!

When purple Jacarandas
Fall from the tree[1]
Be careful! 'Cos they make the path
Very slippery! Whoops![2]

Tell the children that...

Pietermaritzburg is such a long name that it is often called by its 'abbreviated' or shortened name, 'Maritzburg.

Think of other cities with long names that are abbreviated. Clap the rhythms of the names and the abbreviations.

Sound effects

[1] Xylophone glissandi, soft tambourine shake or shakers.
[2] Cymbals clashing together.

Encourage the children to choose their own body percussion for this speech pattern. The rhythm may be performed separately or together.

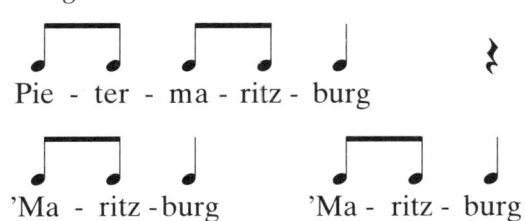

Pie - ter - ma - ritz - burg

'Ma - ritz - burg   'Ma - ritz - burg

NAMAQUALAND DAISIES

Doh: G (Key: G major)

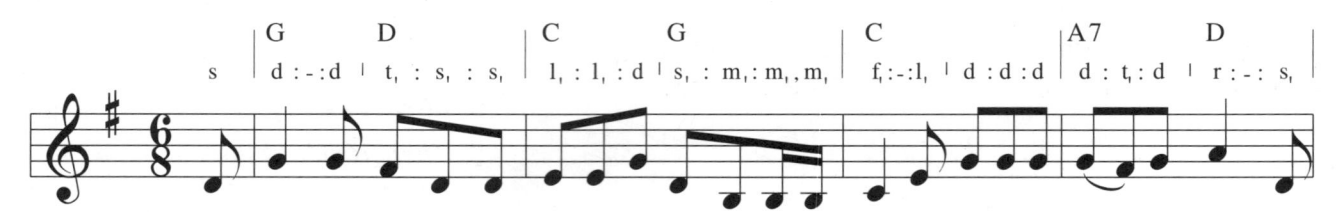

mf In spring the show-ers bring beau-ti-ful flo-wers to the de-sert sand of Na-ma-qua-land. *p* On Mon-day not a flow'r a-ny-where, On Tues-day mil-lions of dai-sies to share!

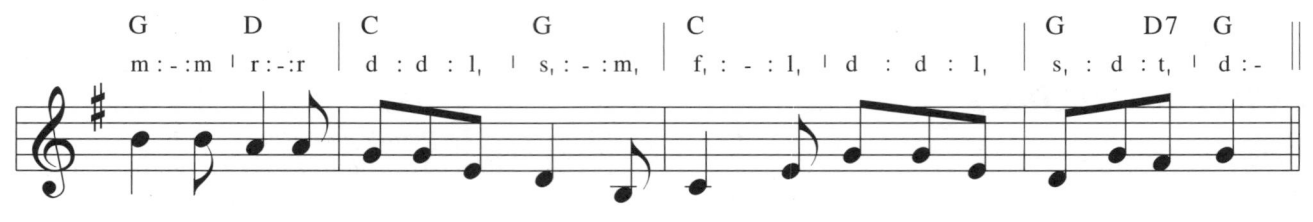

mf

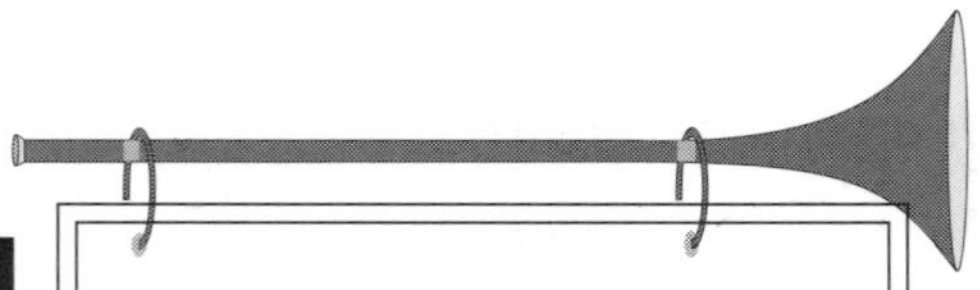

Let's be . . . NAMAQUALAND DAISIES

Group A, 'the flowers', lie quietly on the ground. They rise up, opening their petals to the sky when Group B, 'the showers', stand over the flowers, hands raised, fingers in 'wiggly' rain-like movements.

Group C may also make 'showery sounds', either sh-sh, clicking tongues, Δ tremolo or shaking shakers.

Tell the children that . . .

People come from all over the world to see the wonderful sight of the Namaqualand daisies, which cover huge areas of land.

Mooi Nomsa (Afrikaans)

Nomsa lyk so kleurvol
Met haar kombers so rooi!
Sy dra ook baie kraaltjies
Waarmee sy haar tooi.

Let's be . . . BEADMAKERS

Encourage the children to thread beads or flowers that have fallen on the ground. Azalea and hibiscus flowers thread well.

KIRSTENBOSCH SE WILDEBLOMTUIN
(Afrikaans)

Gentle, swaying rhythm
Doh: F (Key: F major)

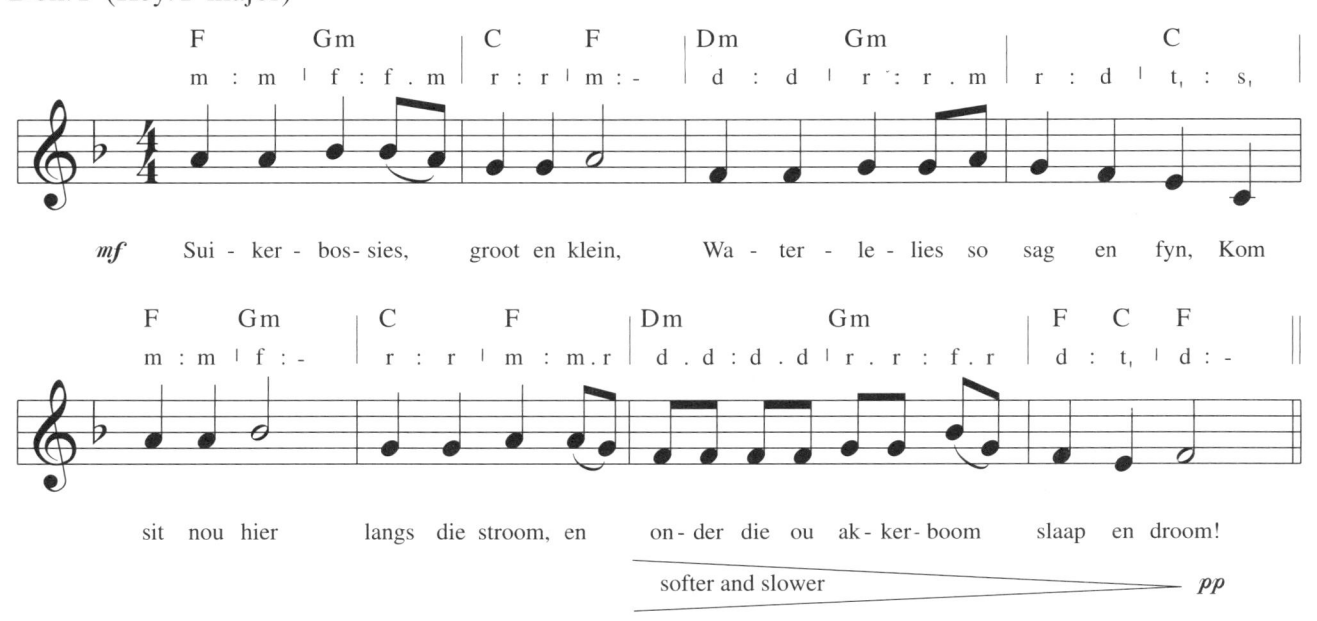

mf Sui - ker - bos - sies, groot en klein, Wa - ter - le - lies so sag en fyn, Kom

sit nou hier langs die stroom, en on - der die ou ak - ker - boom slaap en droom!

softer and slower — *pp*

Ostinato accompaniment (xylophone)

Clap hands softly, close to the ear, in a sleep-like position
slaap en droom

Xylophone glissandi make restful 'watery' sounds.

The Indian Market

Papadums, samoosas,
Curry and rice,
Sambals, chillibites
Herbs and spice.

Incense, ornaments
And silks, so exquisite,
The Indian market
Is the place to visit.

Tell the children that...

The Indian market in Durban is a world of wonderful flavours and fragrances.

Clap clap-together

A fun activity that works well with many poems. The children form pairs, face each other and clap their own hands ♩♩ and their partner's hands ♩

herbs and spice
clap clap clap-together

Lots of scope for imaginative action!

Diamond digging

*From the train window
I can see
The great Big Hole of
Kimberley!*

*Diamonds, diamonds
In the ground
Are there any more
To be found?*

*Diamonds, blue
Diamonds, white
Oh! How they shine,
Bright! bright! bright!*

*Come on, all!
DIG! DIG! DIG!
I'm going to find one!
BIG! BIG! BIG!*

Let's be ... DIAMOND DIGGERS
The repeated words may be stamped while doing a digging movement.

Sugar

*Tiny grains of sugar,
You are so small –
Did you really come
From sugar-cane so tall?*

*At the Sugar Terminal
Machines chopped me
Into smaller pieces
To sweeten your tea.*

*Tiny grains of sugar
You are so small –
Did you really come
From sugar-cane so tall?*

Suiker (Afrikaans)

*Suiker, suiker,
Natalse riet!
Ek sal jou
In my tee geniet!*

Let's be ... THE SUGAR-CANE CHOPPER
Children jump on the spot, chopping the sugar cane with their feet.

Introduction, link and coda

Say and clap

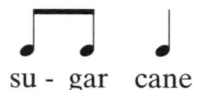

su - gar cane

Ostinato accompaniment

Throughout verse 2

Claves

chop chop

GRAPE FUN!

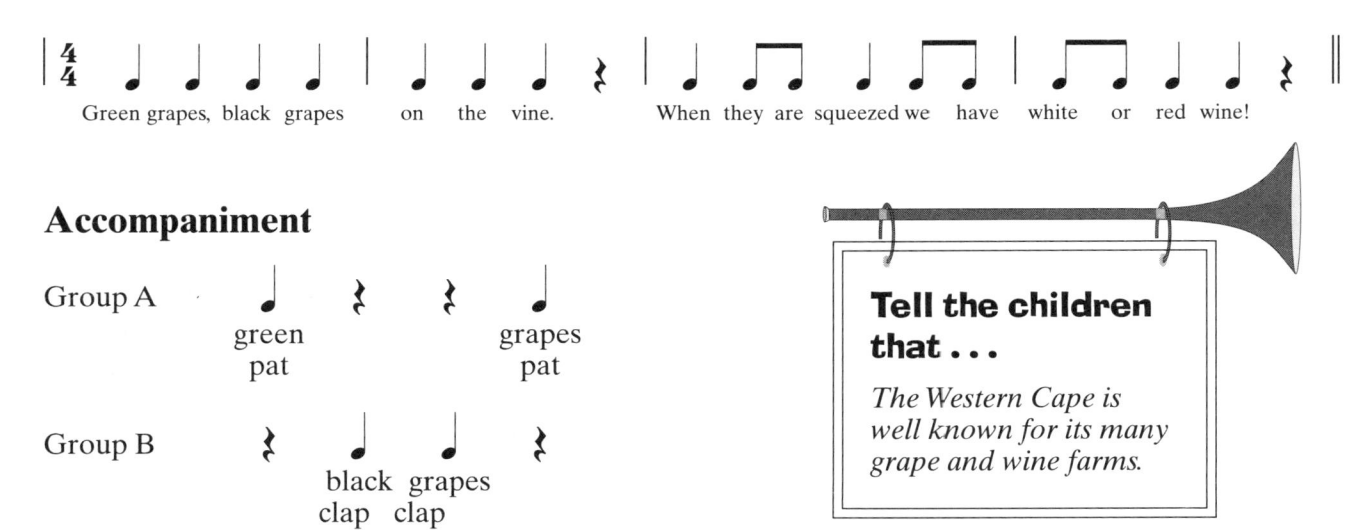

| 4/4 ♩ ♩ ♩ ♩ | ♩ ♩ ♩ 𝄽 | ♩ ♫ ♩ ♫ | ♫ ♩ ♩ 𝄽 ‖

Green grapes, black grapes on the vine. When they are squeezed we have white or red wine!

Accompaniment

Group A   ♩ 𝄽 𝄽 ♩
           green   grapes
           pat   pat

Group B   𝄽 ♩ ♩ 𝄽
              black grapes
              clap clap

This may be done separately or together.

Tell the children that . . .
The Western Cape is well known for its many grape and wine farms.

WHAT IS A RAISIN?

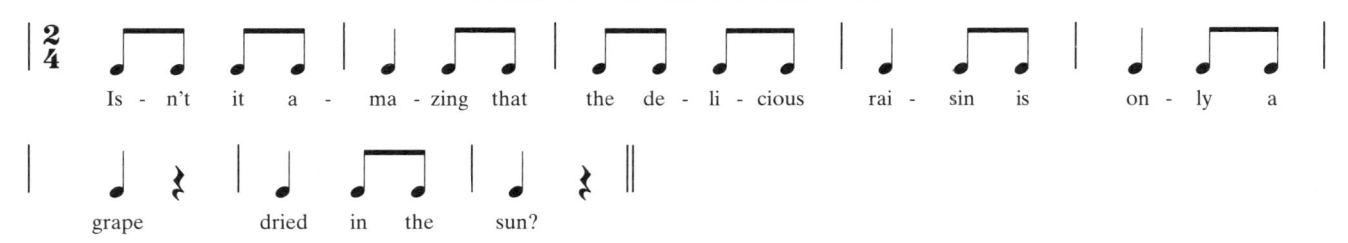

| 2/4 ♫ ♫ | ♩ ♫ | ♫ ♫ | ♩ ♫ | ♩ ♫ |

Is - n't it a - ma - zing that the de - li - cious rai - sin is on - ly a

| ♩ 𝄽 | ♩ ♫ | ♩ 𝄽 ‖

grape dried in the sun?

Accompaniment

Divide the class into three groups..

Group A   Say the poem. Later clap it.

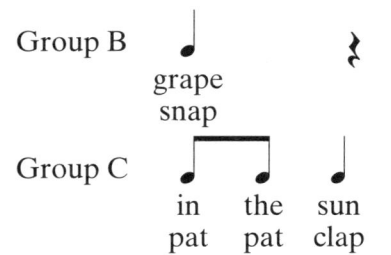

Group B   ♩   𝄽
           grape
           snap

Group C   ♫   ♩
           in the sun
           pat pat clap

All kinds of creatures

HOOPOE

Doh: C (Key: C major)

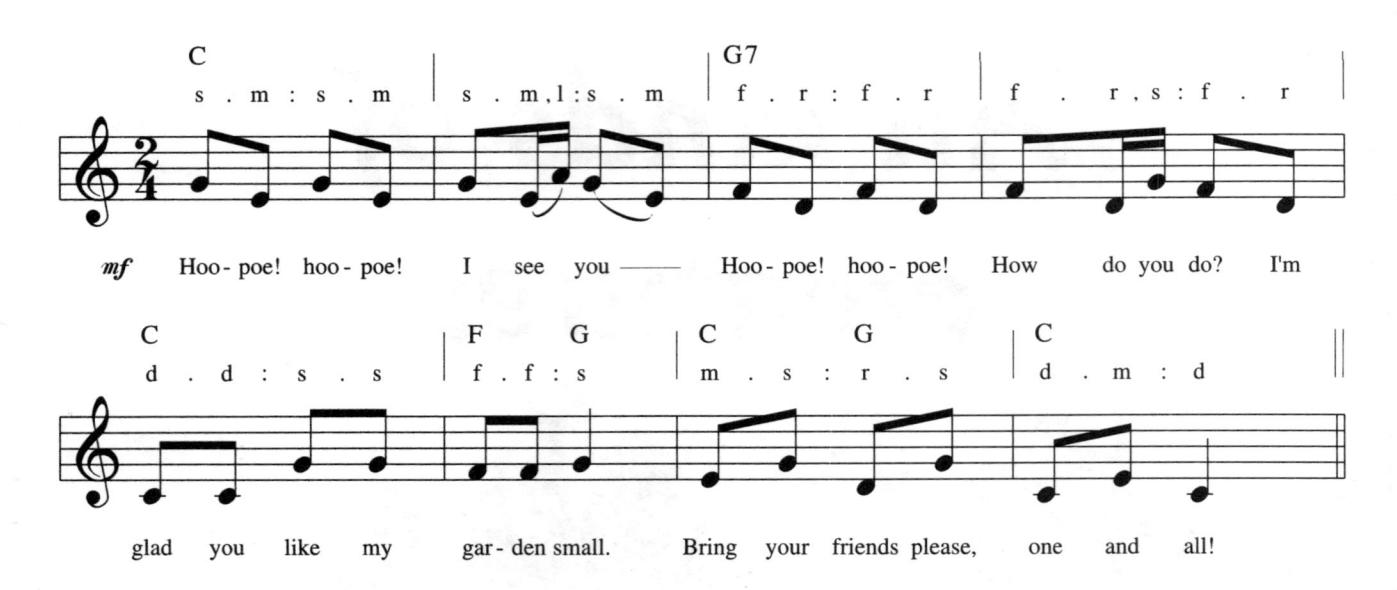

```
      C                              G7
s . m : s . m | s . m , l : s . m | f . r : f . r | f . r , s : f . r |
```

mf Hoo-poe! hoo-poe! I see you — Hoo-poe! hoo-poe! How do you do? I'm

```
  C              F       G      | C       G    | C
d . d : s . s | f . f : s | m . s : r . s | d . m : d ||
```

glad you like my gar-den small. Bring your friends please, one and all!

PIET-MY-VROU
(Afrikaans)

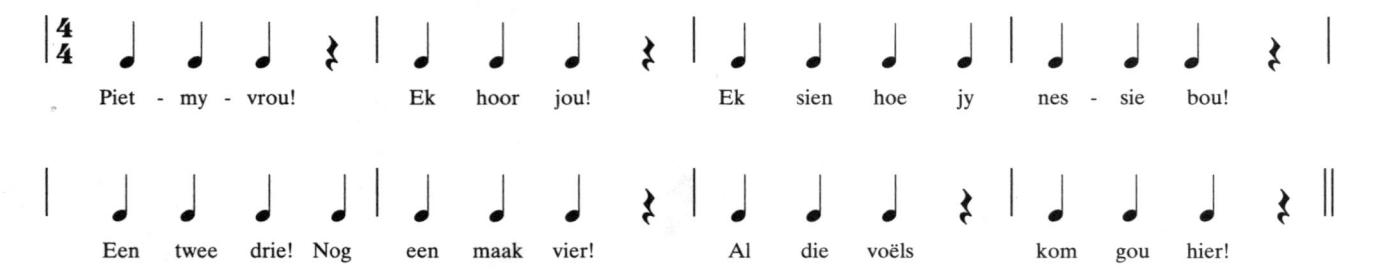

Piet - my - vrou! Ek hoor jou! Ek sien hoe jy nes - sie bou!

Een twee drie! Nog een maak vier! Al die voëls kom gou hier!

Accompaniment

Bars 1 and 2, 7 and 8

          voël - tjie
1   2   3   clap pat

DIE HADEDA
(Afrikaans)

Cheekily
Doh: F (Key: F major)

F		C			F
s, . d : d . d	d . t, : t, . t,	s, . r : r . r	r . d , d : d

Waar-om kla die ha-de-da? Hy kla vir sy ma, hy kla vir sy pa!

		C7		F		C		F
m . m : s . s	s . f : r . f , f	m . d , d : r . t,	d . m : d

nê nê nê nê nê nê nê Ha-de-da, ha-de-da, Wat wil jy hê?

In a nasal way...

Sound effects

Bars 5 and 6   Copy the raucous, nasal sound of the hadeda by holding your nose while singing.

BIRD TALK

An echo-song
Doh: C (Pentatonic C)

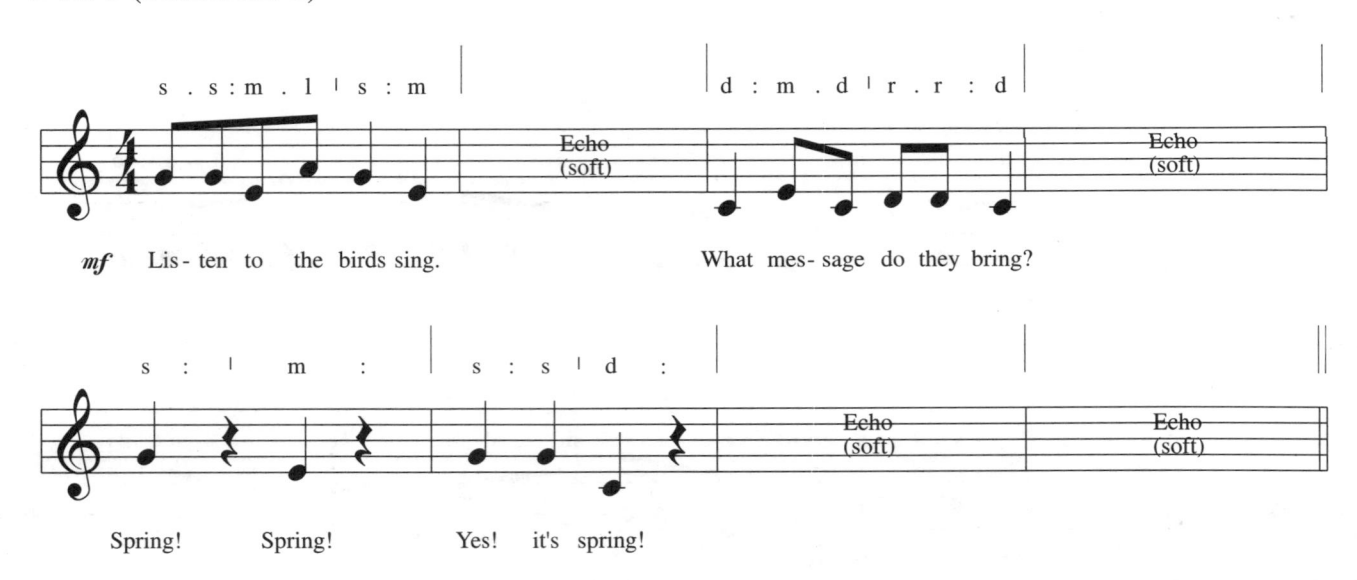

```
s . s : m . l | s : m  ||  d : m . d | r . r : d
```

mf Lis-ten to the birds sing.   Echo (soft)   What mes-sage do they bring?   Echo (soft)

```
s : | m : | s : s | d :
```

Spring!   Spring!   Yes! it's spring!   Echo (soft)   Echo (soft)

🎓 *The echo is soft and may be clapped, sung to 'lah' or whistled.*

Accompaniment

Bars 5 and/or 6 may be repeated on chime bars or glockenspiel as an ostinato throughout the song.

Can all birds fly?

Peculiar birds

All: We are the birds
          Who just can't fly!
          We don't know why
          So we'll sit down and cry!*

          Boo-hoo-hoo
          It's not fair!
          Look at the others
          Up in the air!*

Ostrich: I don't care
          What other birds do!
          I like being different!
          How about you?*

All: Maybe you're right!
          We're sure you are!
          It's much more fun
          Being pe-cu-li-ar!*

* Stamp after the word.

> **Tell the children that . . .**
>
> *It's not only the ostrich that is 'peculiar'. Encourage the children to think of other birds that cannot fly.*

🎓 *Choose a rhythmic pattern from the poem. Use it as a body percussion link between the verses.*

e.g. ♪ ♩ ♪ ♩
     sit down and cry

KOKKEWIET SE LIED

Brightly (Afrikaans)
Doh: D (Key: D major)

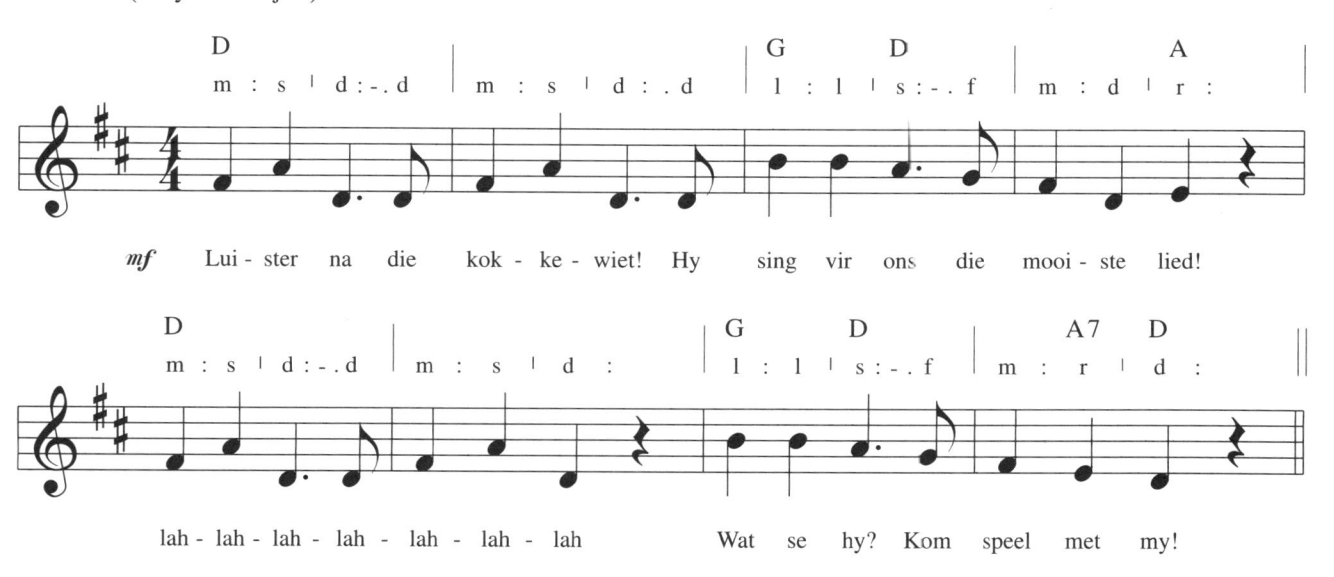

mf Lui - ster na die kok - ke - wiet! Hy sing vir ons die mooi - ste lied!

lah - lah - lah - lah - lah - lah - lah   Wat se hy? Kom speel met my!

Sound effects

Bars 3 and 4, 7 and 8   Triangle tremolo

and/or

Bars 1 and 2, 5 and 6   Glockenspiel

Kok - ke - wiet!
L   R   L

Penguin

The penguin waddles
On two webbed feet –
Quite the strangest bird to meet!

However hard he may try,
This is a bird
That will never fly!

Let's be . . . PENGUINS

The children waddle, lurching slightly from side to side. Babies often waddle when they start to walk.

Introduction, accompaniment and coda

Clap or stamp
two webbed feet

75

Volstruis (Afrikaans)

Hoor jy
Hoe hy
Ons bedrieg?
Volstruis is 'n voël
Maar, kan hy vlieg?
NEE!

🎓 *The teacher or a group of children may say the poem and all join in with an emphatic 'NEE'.*

A rhythmic poem with a question and answer.

Fruit bat

Tat-tat-tat
Tat-tat-tat!
What sound is that?
It's the fruit bat!
Tat-tat-tat
Tat-tat-tat!

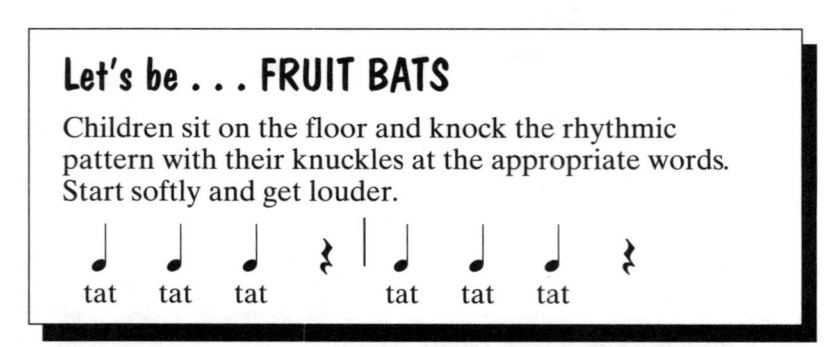

Let's be . . . FRUIT BATS
Children sit on the floor and knock the rhythmic pattern with their knuckles at the appropriate words. Start softly and get louder.

tat tat tat   tat tat tat

🎓 *Divide the class into three groups.*

  Group A   Lines 1 and 2, 5 and 6
  Group B   Line 3
  Group C   Line 4

'Tat-tats' may be knocked, spoken or played on claves or woodblock.

Isikhukhukazi (Zulu)

Isikhukhukazi
Sizalela amaqanda
Ke-kê-ka, ke-kê-ka

The hen (Translated from Zulu)

The hen
Lays eggs
Cluck-cluck-cluck

Iinyosi (Xhosa)

Sibulela iinyosi
Xa sitya ubusi

The bees (Translated from Xhosa)

We thank the bees
When we eat honey

Sound effects

A group of children may buzz 'z-z-z' while the poem is spoken.

A poem with contrasting moods, dynamics and speeds.

Spider

She sits so calmly,
Spinning her thread
To make a pretty, cosy web.

But do not be misled –
That web will hold you
'Til you're dead!

Introduction

Clap — spin-ning her thread

Coda

Stamp — 'Til you're dead!

Let's be ... SPIDERS

Verse 1:
Sway in time or move your hands in a circular spinning-wheel action. The left hand may 'hold the spindle' in an upright clutched position, while the right hand makes a circular movement.

Snakes

Snakes slither and slide and are sly and snide. If I saw one I should hide. For I wouldn'nt like to be in his inside!

Sound effects

Body: Rub palms of hands together to make the s-s-s sound.
Speech: Hiss-s-s throughout the poem.
Instruments: Shakers or tambourines shaken throughout the poem.

Clear diction adds to the mood of the poem. Emphasise the words 'slide', 'snide', 'hide', 'inside', and the hissing sounds of the 's' words.

Tell the children that ...

'Slither' and 'slide' are 'creeping' words! Children enjoy creating their own creeping words.

Children find the story of the coelacanth as exciting as that of dinosaurs.

Coelacanth

The coelacanth gave us all a surprise
When he swam along our coast –
He hadn't been seen for millions of years
Now he definitely isn't a ghost!

🎓 *Coelacanth is a new word for most children. Make it into a speech pattern.*

Say and pat

coe - la - canth

Let's be . . . FISH

Fish feel slippery. As children say 'coelacanth', they slide their hands together, up and down.

Introduction, accompaniment and coda

Group A say and clap

coe - la - canth

Group B say and pat

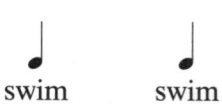

swim   swim

Group C say the poem.

When the groups can clap and pat their patterns with ease, they may do them simultaneously. Encourage the children to decide on their own percussion, e.g.

coe - la - canth
pat   pat   clap

or   △   △   cymbals

or

swim   swim
stamp   snap
drum   drum

Tell the children that...

There is coelacanth at the East London museum as well as in the JLB Smith Institute, Rhodes University, Grahamstown. A coelacanth is often called 'Old Four Legs' because the fins look like legs.

No place for a fish

Goodness gracious me!
Where are the fish in the sea?
Plastic bottles and old tin cans,
Broken bicycles, pots and pans
People think it's a rubbish bin!
Where on earth can a fish
Flap a fin?

🎓 *Children enjoy the sound of music made by filling glasses with varying amounts of water and playing them gently with a padded beater or flicked finger.*
Glissandi on xylophones or glockenspiels give a watery sound too.

Lady Dimple

The Oceanarium
Is where I want to go,
To see Lady Dimple
At the Dolphin Show.

She can sing
She can count
She can do 'most anything!
The oldest dolphin of them all
Is everyone's favourite,
Big or small!

The Oceanarium
Is where I want to stay
And play with Lady Dimple
Every single day.

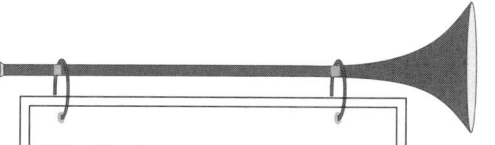

Tell the children that...

Lady Dolphin is a very famous dolphin who lives at the Oceanarium in Port Elizabeth. She is so popular with the Port Elizabeth people and visitors to the city that she was given an award, the only creature ever to have received this honour.

Let's have 'a whale of a time'!

THE WHALE

With a lazy lilt
Doh: B♭ (Key: G minor)

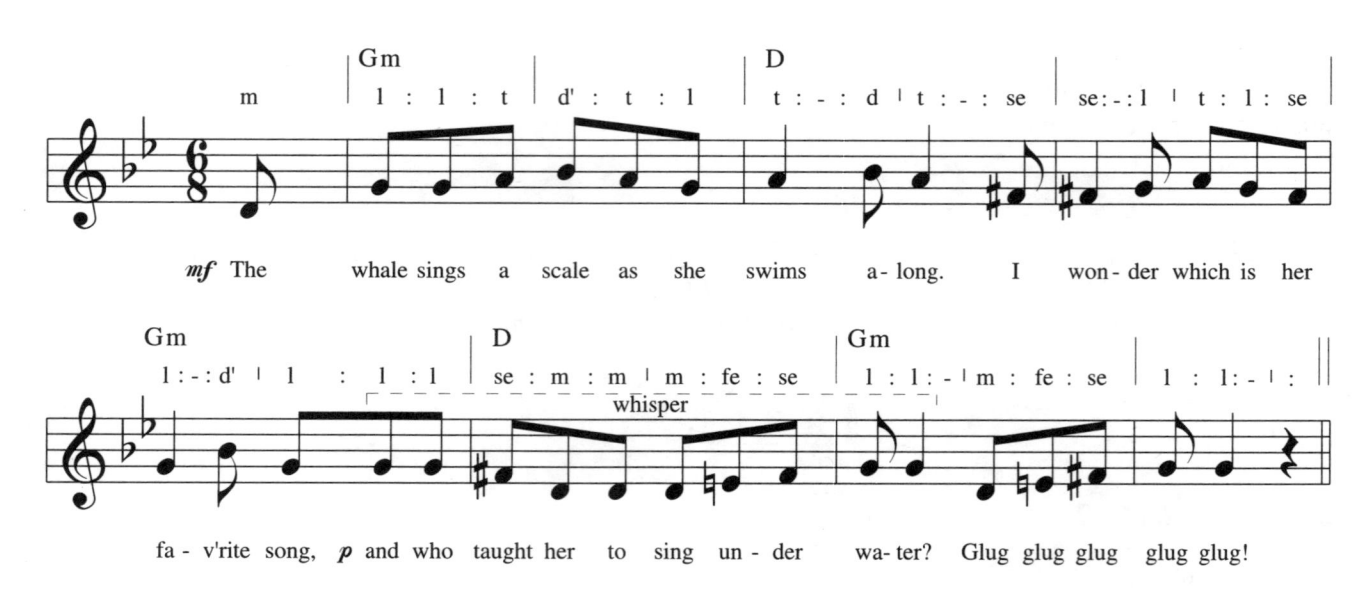

```
         Gm                    D
     m  | l : l : t | d' : t : l | t : - : d | t : - : se | se : - : l | t : l : se
```

mf The whale sings a scale as she swims a-long. I won-der which is her

```
    Gm                D                    Gm
  | l : - : d' | l : l : l | se : m : m | m : fe : se | l : l : - m : fe : se | l : l : - l : ||
                                    whisper
```

fa-v'rite song, *p* and who taught her to sing un-der wa-ter? Glug glug glug glug glug!

Introduction (chime bars or metallophone)

L L L R R

Let's be ... WHALES
Children walk slowly, making large swimming movements with their arms.

Tell the children that ...
A whale 'sings'. Encourage the children to make 'whale sounds'. People have recorded whale sounds which don't sound like our singing, but do sound like music. Try to find a recording at your local music library.

Whisper very softly or you'll spoil the surprise!

THE KRUGER NATIONAL PARK

Doh: F (Key: F major)

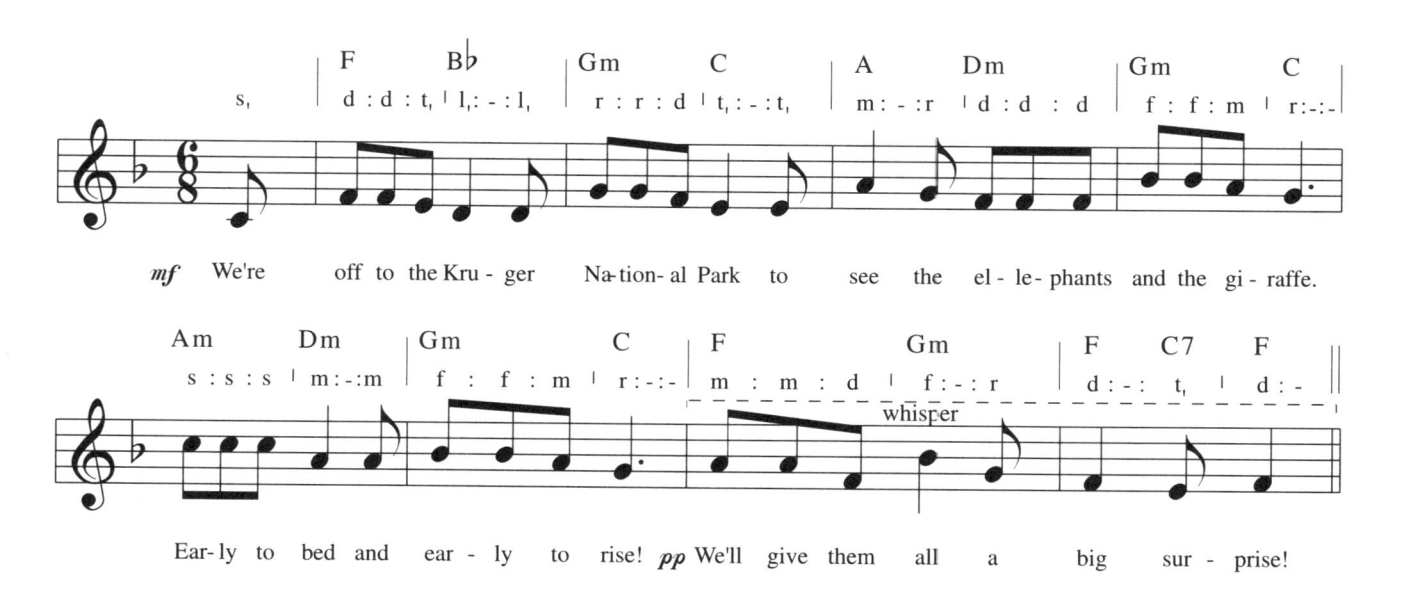

mf We're off to the Kru-ger Na-tion-al Park to see the el-le-phants and the gi-raffe.
Ear-ly to bed and ear-ly to rise! *pp* We'll give them all a big sur-prise!

Accompaniment (tambourine)

Tambourines ♪ 𝄾 𝄾 ♪ 𝄾 𝄾 throughout.
                park   park

DIE NAGAPIE
(Afrikaans)

Happy and light
Doh: C (Key: C major)

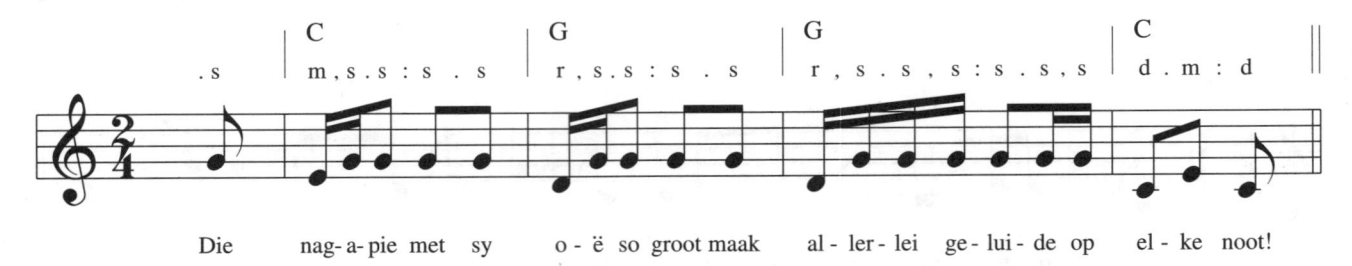

```
       |C            |G            |G              |C
 .s  | m .s,s : s .s | r,.s,s : s .s | r,.s .s,s : s .s,s | d .m : d ||
```

Die nag-a-pie met sy o - ë so groot maak al - ler - lei ge - lui - de op el - ke noot!

Ostinato accompaniment (xylophone)

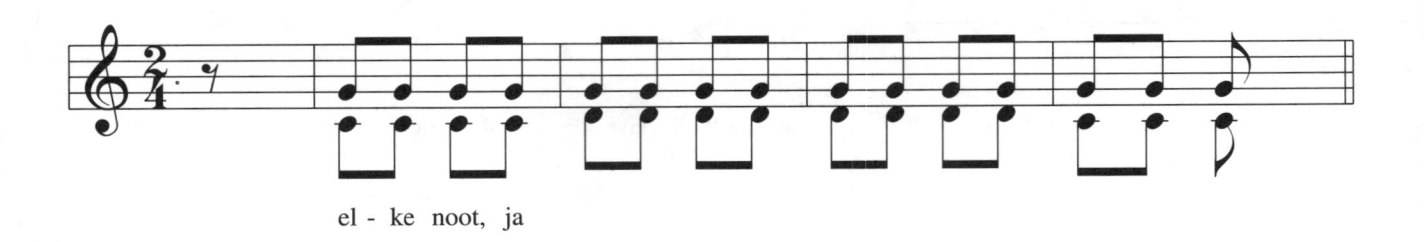

el - ke noot, ja

Introduction and last bar (chime bars)

el - ke noot
L   R   L

Speech pattern

'Allerlei geluide' may be a tongue-twister for some children. Make it into a speech pattern.

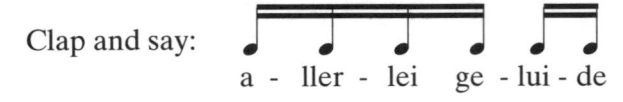

Clap and say: a - ller - lei ge - lui - de

🎓 *Exaggerate the mouth shape. A wide smiling position for 'allerlei ge', pursed lips for 'lui' then smile again for 'de'. The children enjoy copying you and will then pronounce the words correctly.*

Each year the tears flow at silkworm time ... This song reminds the children to feed their pets.

SILKWORM TIME!

With much expression
Doh: G (Key: G major)

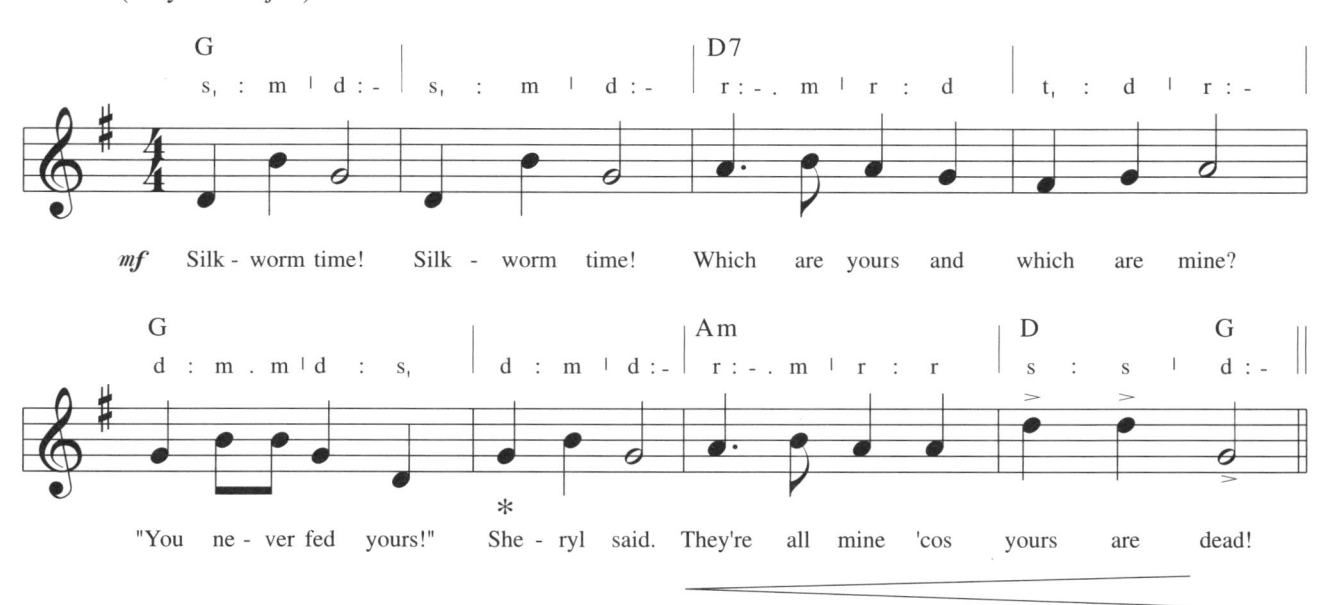

mf Silk - worm time! Silk - worm time! Which are yours and which are mine?

"You ne - ver fed yours!" She - ryl said. They're all mine 'cos yours are dead!

*Substitute a child's name.

Accompaniment (teacher or children) (xylophone)

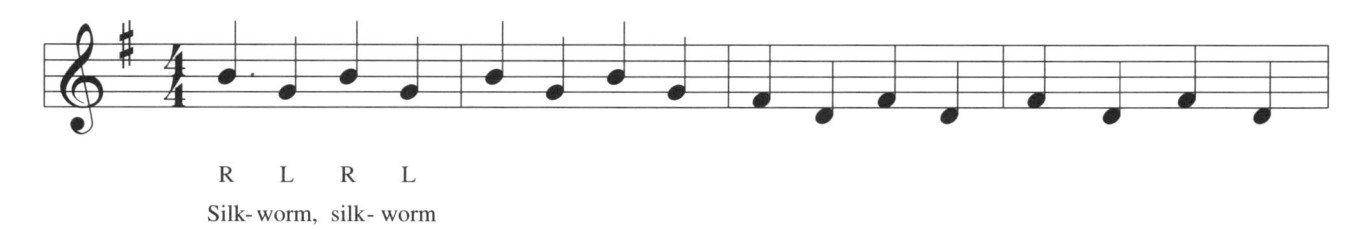

R L R L
Silk-worm, silk-worm

Body percussion accompaniment in pairs:

Bars 1 and 2
silk - worm time
clap   clap   clap-together

Bars 3 to 7   Point at each other at the appropriate words.

Bar 8
yours are   dead
clap   clap clap-together

A song for whispering and laughing.

HYENAS

Slowly, mysteriously
Doh: F (Key: D minor)

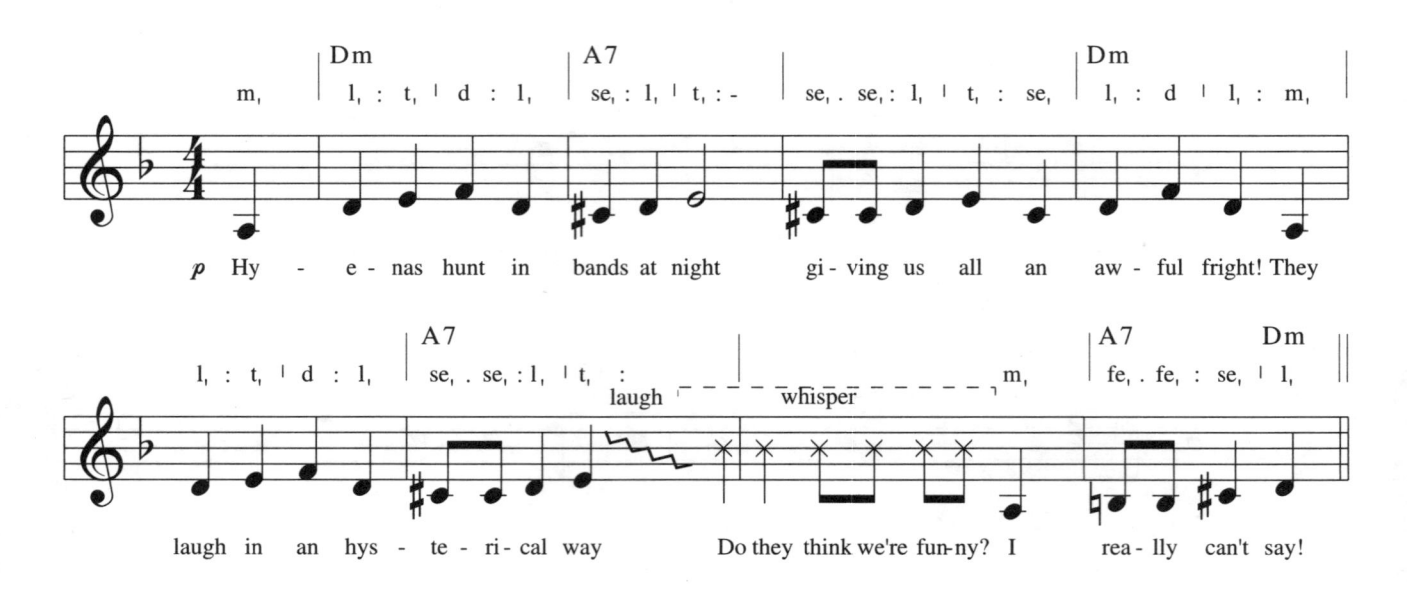

p Hy-e-nas hunt in bands at night giving us all an awful fright! They laugh in an hys-te-ri-cal way Do they think we're fun-ny? I rea-lly can't say!

Let's be ... HYENAS

Children crawl quietly on all fours. They will also enjoy making strange laughs! A xylophone glissando is effective.

Dintja tsa me (Sesotho)

Ke na le dintja tse pedi
Ke na le e kgolo[1]
Ke na le enyane[2]
Ke a di rata.

My dogs (Translated from Sesotho)

I have two dogs
One is big
One is small
I love them.

Sound effects

Children make low[1] and high[2] barking sounds.

RATEL
(Afrikaans)

Doh: C (Key: C major)

```
    C              G7                                              C
    d :m | s :m  | f . f:-.m | r :-  | t, . t,: r . r | f : r | . m:-. r | d :-  ||
```

Ra- tel, ra - tel, kom eet met my! Ek hou ook van heu-ning van die by!

Ostinato accompaniment

Claves or woodblock   ♩ ♩ ♩ ♩
                      ra - tel ra - tel

Rhinoceros

Rhinoceros is NOT a beauty.
His horns are there to do their duty.
If he doesn't like your looks
He'll ram you down
With his own two hooks!

Introduction and coda

Clap   ♩   ♩   ♩   𝄽
or
woodblock   own two hooks

Let's be . . . RHINOS

Place left wrist on forehead with fingers together pointing forward. Place right wrist on chin with fingers together pointing forward. Walk with slow and heavy steps.

85

This staccato song needs clear diction.

ZEBRA

At a steady, trotting pace
Doh: D (Key: D major)

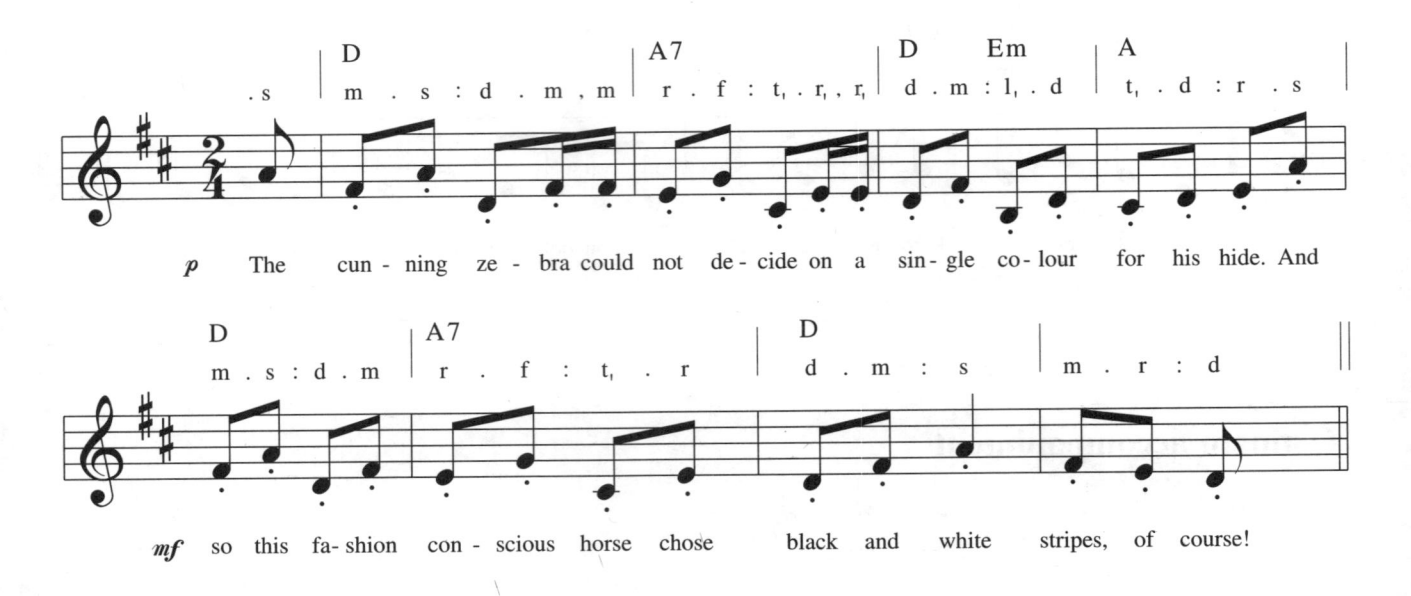

p The cun-ning ze-bra could not de-cide on a sin-gle co-lour for his hide. And

mf so this fa-shion con-scious horse chose black and white stripes, of course!

Ostinato accompaniment (hand bells)

Hand bells ♩♩ ♩ throughout.

ze - bra stripes

Musical concepts

The songs, poems and speech patterns in this section focus on particular concepts:

sound and silence
high and low
fast and slow
staccato (detached notes) and legato (joined notes)
loud and soft

Sound and silence

The rests indicate silent beats.

STOP STREETS

Rhythmic and bright
Doh: F (Key: F major)

[Musical notation with lyrics:]
mf Toot-toot-toot! Here we are! In my bright red mo-tor car!
At the stop street I must stop, or be fined by a traf-fic cop!

Encourage the children to choose their favourite colour, in place of red.

Sound effects

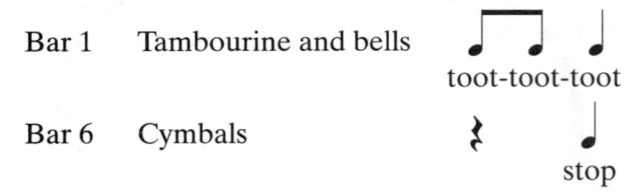

Bar 1   Tambourine and bells
        toot-toot-toot

Bar 6   Cymbals
        stop

Let's be ... DRIVERS

The children are cars on the road. The teacher plays a ♩ beat or ♪ pattern on the hand drum and the 'cars' move accordingly.

car car   or   zoom-zoom zoom-zoom

When the drum stops the 'cars' must stop.

TRAFFIC LIGHTS

Doh: F (Key: F major)

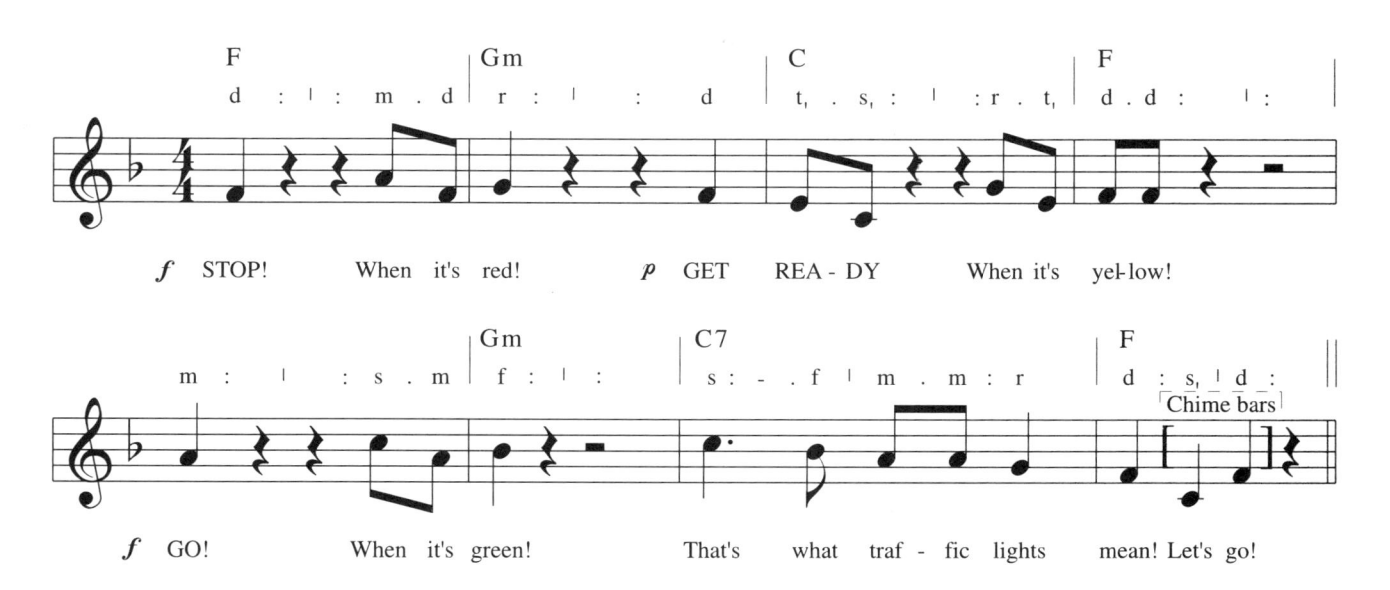

f STOP! When it's red! *p* GET REA-DY When it's yel-low!

f GO! When it's green! That's what traf-fic lights mean! Let's go!

Accompaniment

Divide the accompaniment into three groups.

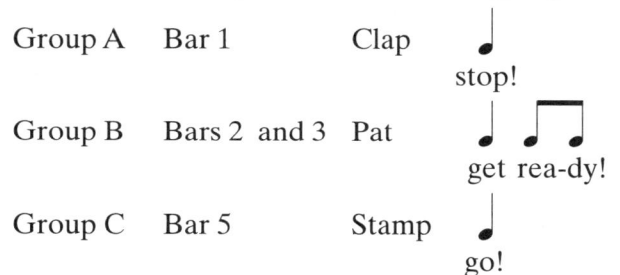

Group A	Bar 1	Clap	stop!
Group B	Bars 2 and 3	Pat	get rea-dy!
Group C	Bar 5	Stamp	go!
All	Bars 7 and 8	Clap, pat and stamp the rhythmic pattern.

Tell the children that...

Rests are silent beats. Count them silently.

Verkeersligte (Afrikaans)

'Hou stil!' sê rooi
'Kyk!' sê geel
'Beweeg!' sê groen
Die verkeersligte beveel!

Let's be... TRAFFIC LIGHTS

Divide the class into three groups, wearing red, yellow or green paper crowns. Each group says the words appropriate to their colour.

Line 1: Children stand with hands in 'stop' position.
Line 2: 'Cup' the hands around the eyes, like binoculars.
Line 3 and 4: March on the spot.

High and low

The melody rises to its high note.

THE POSTBOX

Doh: C (Key: C major)

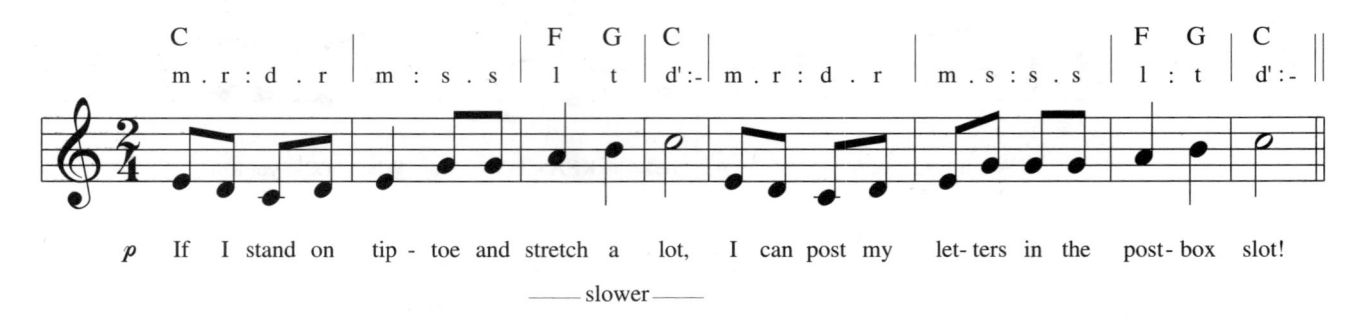

C		F G C		F G C
m . r : d . r	m : s . s	l : t | d' :-	m . r : d . r	m : s . s	l : t | d' :-

p If I stand on tip-toe and stretch a lot, I can post my let-ters in the post-box slot!

———— slower ————

🎓 *Stand the xylophone on its base, and play the melody so that the children can 'see' the notes ascending. The children draw the ascending line of the melody to 'see' that the melody rises.*

The teacher may draw an ascending line on the blackboard and let each child stretch to reach the final 'notes'.

Tell the children that...

They must listen carefully when you sing the song and then decide if the melody is repeated.

Why can't I?

Why can't I
Fly high
In the sky?
A bird
Doesn't even
Have to try!

Accompaniment

Children clap hands above their heads throughout the poem: ♩ ♩ ♩ 𝄽
                                                              Why can't I?

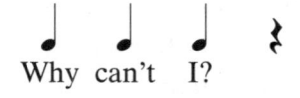

The melody, like the mole, descends.

MOLE

Doh: C (Key: C Major)

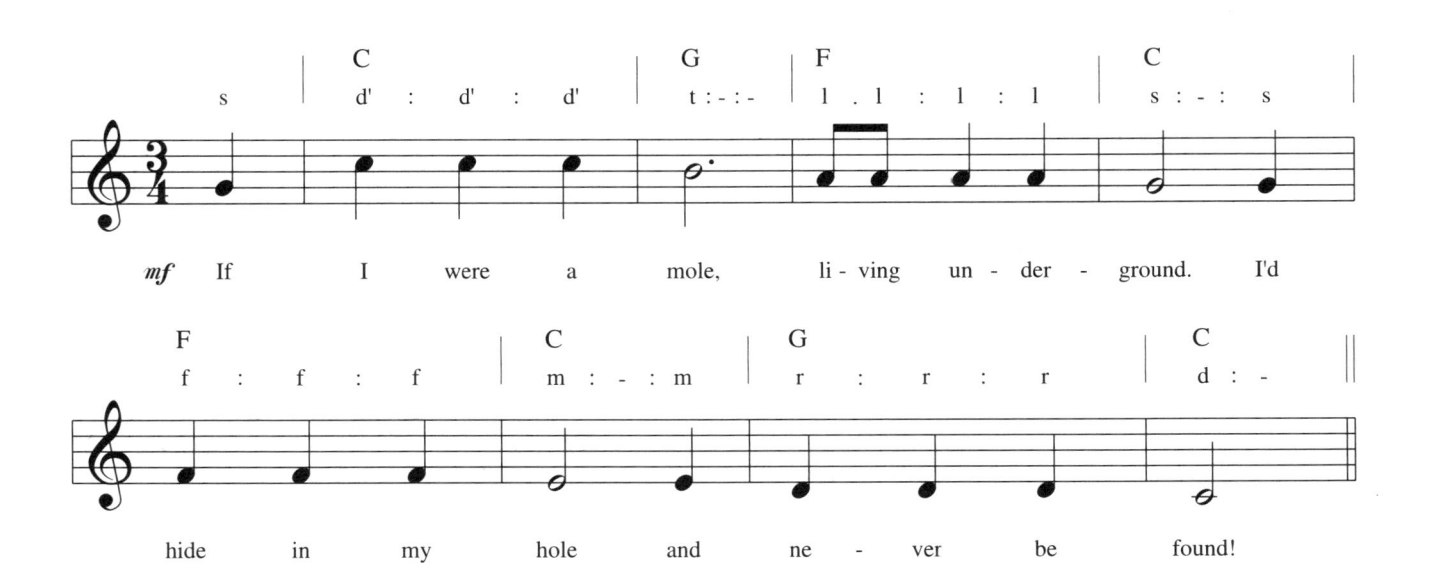

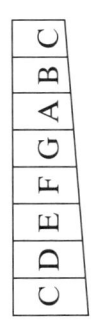

	C			G	F		C
s	d' : d' : d'	t : - : -	l . l : l : l	s : - : s

mf If I were a mole, li - ving un - der - ground. I'd

F	C	G	C
f : f : f	m : - : m	r : r : r	d : -

hide in my hole and ne - ver be found!

Xylophone bars: C D E F G A B C

🎓 *Hold the xylophone in an upright position. Play the melody on the xylophone so that the children can see how the melody descends.*

Let's be ... MOLES

The teacher plays the melody on an inverted xylophone. The children stand, then gradually bend lower and lower until curled up on the floor.

Up and down the xylophone ladder

One step, two steps
Three steps, four.
Slide down the ladder,
But don't get sore!

Five, six, seven,
Eight, nine, ten.
Higher and higher.
Then VROOPS! Down again!

Let's be . . . CLIMBERS

Make ascending 'steps' in the air with your hands, then a quick descending 'slide' at the appropriate words. The teacher may play ascending and descending notes on the inverted xylophone so that the children can see and hear the 'steps'.

Gardening

First the seed I must sow
Then I wait for it to grow . . .
Lots of water for it to drink –
It must be full by now, I think.
Oh! What fun! There's the sun!
Look, everyone! My radish is done!

Divide the class into three groups:
  Group A   The 'seeds', lie curled up, asleep in their own 'space'.
  Group B   The 'gardeners' 'water' the seeds, which uncurl and stretch when
  Group C   the 'sun' appears.

Let's be . . . 'REAL' GARDENERS

Make the poem come true! Sow radish or bean seeds in wet cotton wool, transfer them to soil when they have sprouted. Follow the poem's instructions and wait patiently. If the children say the poem to their seed, it may grow even faster . . .

The sun sets at the end of the day. This song also illustrates the concept of fairly loud to very soft.

LALA KAHLE
(Zulu)

Doh: C (Key: C major)

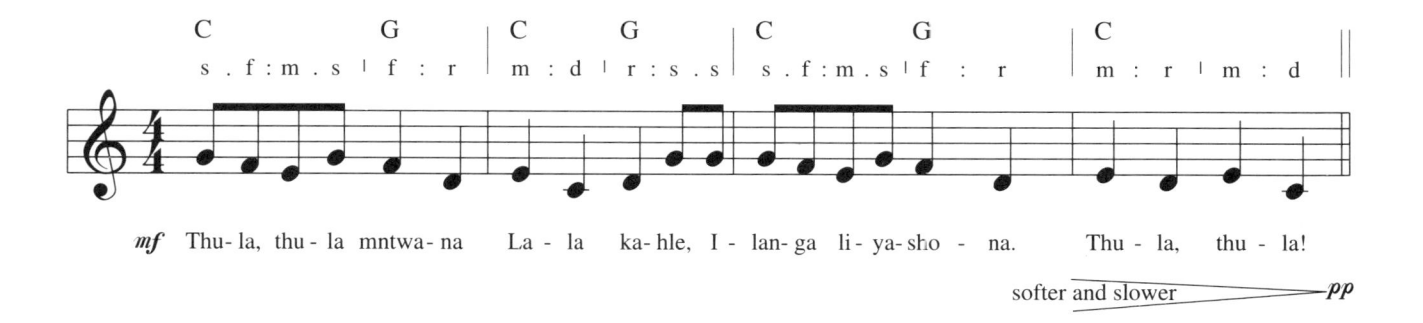

mf Thu-la, thu-la mntwa-na La-la ka-hle, I-lan-ga li-ya-sho-na. Thu-la, thu-la!

softer and slower ——— *pp*

Go to sleep *(Translated from Zulu)*

Be quiet, be quiet my baby
Go to sleep,
The sun is setting
Be quiet, be quiet.

Ostinato accompaniment (hand bells, triangle)

Hand bells or △ ♩ 𝄽 ♩ 𝄽

The teacher, or one child facing the class, does the above activity. The class, who are standing up, gradually sink to the floor as the 'sun' sets.

Let's be ... SETTING SUNS
The children paint pictures of the sun or cut out a circle of cardboard, painted yellow. They hold the 'sun' in one hand, arm outstretched above their heads. They gradually move the 'sun' in a semicircular position down to their knees.

Farmer Forbes says that we may pick avocado pears from his tree and also those that have fallen on the ground. But he will tell us which are the best ones! The teacher, and later a child, makes high and low speech, vocal or instrumental sounds, and the children stretch and bend down accordingly.

Avocado pears

*Avocado pears
On the tree,
I stretch and stretch
But you're too high for me!*

*Look! Oh look!
What I have found!
Avocado pears
Lying on the ground!*

Some for Dad,   (stretch)
And some for me!   (bend low)
*What a generous
Avocado pear tree!*

Fast and slow

Cheetah

*The fastest animal
Is the cheetah,
In a four-legged race
NO-ONE can beat her.
Take your marks!
Get set! Go!
The cheetah's won!
We're all too slow!*

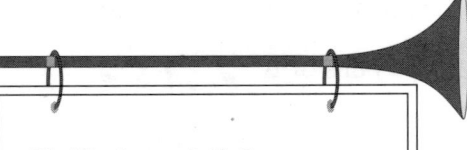

Tell the children that . . .

Some creatures have more than four legs, some have fewer and some have none at all! (Refer to the appropriate songs and poems.)

Play fast and slow music. The children decide whether the music represents cheetahs or snails. Encourage the children to make their own sounds for the rest of the class to decide whether they are fast or slow creatures.

Children experience the concepts of high and low in the actions of this song.

THE OSTRICH

Doh: G (Key: G major)

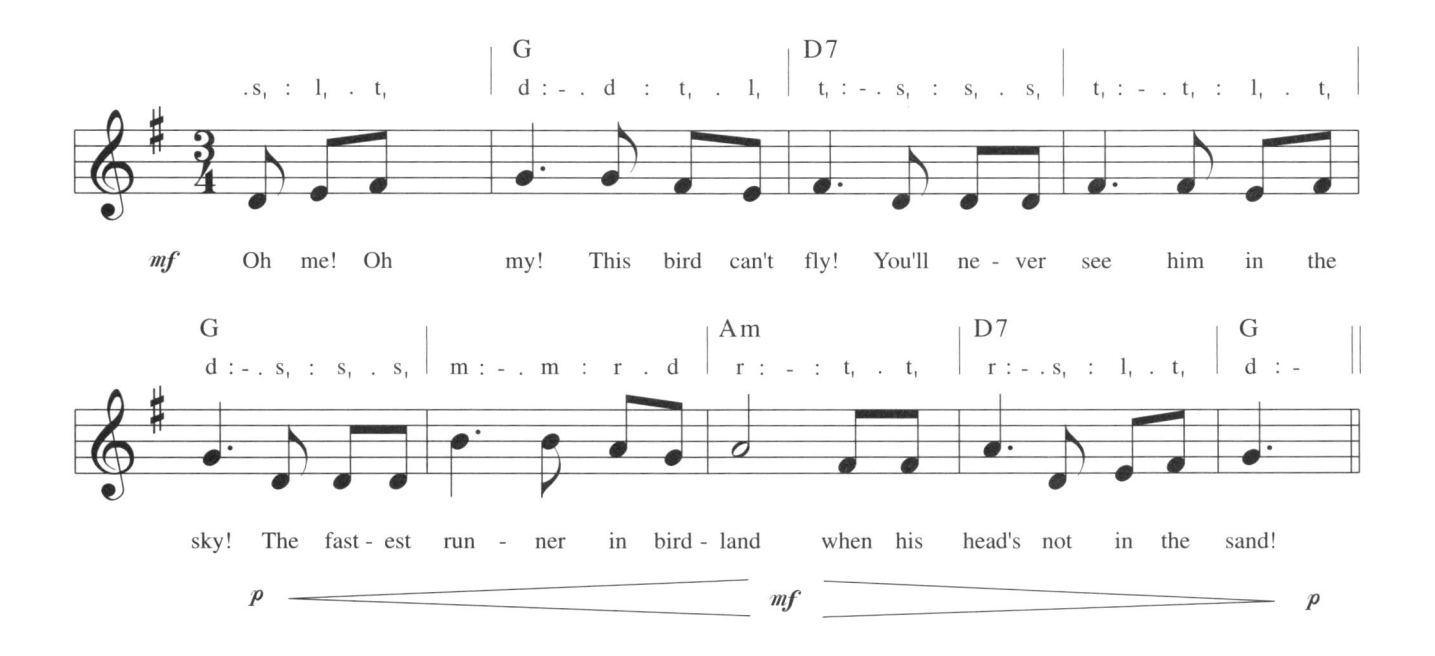

mf Oh me! Oh my! This bird can't fly! You'll ne-ver see him in the sky! The fast-est run-ner in bird-land when his head's not in the sand!

p ——— *mf* ——— *p*

Let's be . . . OSTRICHES

Form a circle. One child, 'the ostrich' stands in the middle. The children sing the song, pointing at the 'ostrich', 'sky' and 'sand' at the appropriate time.

The 'ostrich' tries to flap its wings (arms) and sadly shakes its head. It then bends its body so that its bottom is up and head 'in the sand'. Finally it runs out of the circle.

All pout lips to resemble an ostrich beak! Place hands on hips, elbows out. Move elbows (wings) forward and backward pretending to fly.

Tell the children that . . .

Oudtshoorn is famous for its ostriches. Ostrich feathers were once very fashionable on hats, dresses and as fans. They are still used for feather dusters.

Do the children know that the ostrich is the biggest bird and that ostrich eggs are the biggest eggs in the world?

The ostrich doesn't dig its head in the sand. Instead, it stretches its neck along the ground so that it is difficult for an enemy to see it, as its colour blends with the scenery.

Use the 'Postman's Song' to encourage the children to experience the concepts of fast and slow, heavy and light.

POSTMAN'S SONG

Doh: F (Key: F major)

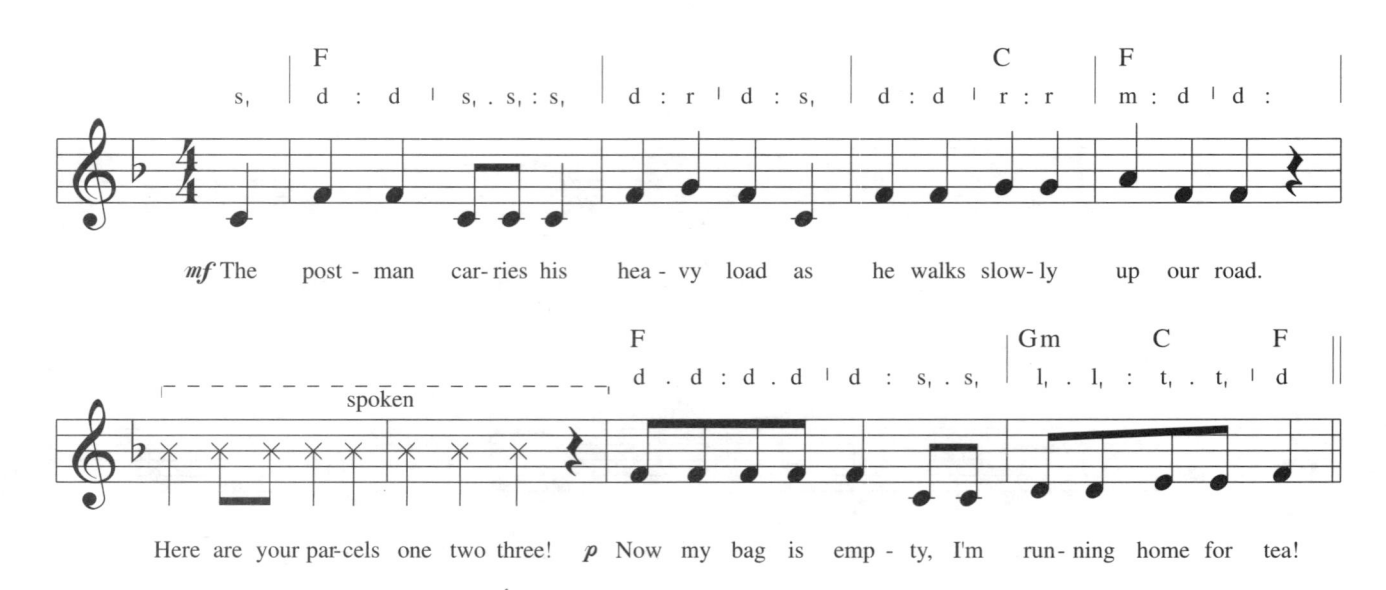

mf The post-man car-ries his hea-vy load as he walks slow-ly up our road.

spoken: Here are your par-cels one two three! *p* Now my bag is emp-ty, I'm run-ning home for tea!

Accompaniment

Bar 6 Drum one two three

Bar 8 Triangle run-ning home for tea

Let's be ... POSTMEN

This activity may be enjoyed with or without the song.

Three children choose their 'own places' in the room. They are the 'postboxes'. The 'postman' walks slowly, with heavy steps, delivers a parcel to each one, then runs lightly 'home'.

The snail moves slowly but steadily.

Our snail

*He cannot run
This snail of ours
A short walk takes him
Simply hours!*

*He'll never win
A running race –
Slow and steady
Is his pace.*

*I don't mind
If he takes his time,
'Cos this slimy snail
Is a friend of mine.*

A poem with a moral! It includes the concepts of fast and slow, loud and soft.

Hasie en skilpad (Afrikaans)

*Hasie! Hasie!
Kom gou hier!
Jy dink jy is
Die slimste dier.*

*Hasie! Hasie!
Is dit waar?
Daar wen skilpad
Die resie klaar.*

*Hasie! Hasie!
Waarom gegaap?
Jy het wraggies
Op pad geslaap!*

We must move quickly to catch the train.

Gijima! Gijima! (Zulu)

*Gijima! Gijima!
Isitimela siyakushiya
Gijima! Gijima!
Uzosala.*

Hurry! Hurry! (Translated from Zulu)

*Hurry! Hurry!
The train is leaving you behind
Hurry! Hurry!
You will remain.*

Sound effects

The poem invites sound effects during or after each line.

Line 1 and 3   Clap or click   Gi - ji - ma! Gi - ji - ma!

Line 2   Whistle or 'hoot'.

Line 4   Stamp   u - zo - sa - la

Encourage the children to create their own sounds and ideas.

This poem, like the trains, moves at various speeds.

Trains

The Banana Express puffs along
Chuffing its happy steam-train song.
Refrain: *Chuff-a-long! Chuff-a-long! Chuff-a-long!*

The Orange Express steaks ahead
Stopping only when the signal's red.
Refrain: *Streaks ahead! Streaks ahead! Streaks ahead!*
                             (getting gradually faster)

My favourite is the suburban train
'All stations please! Alle stasies, asseblief!'*
Stop start, stop start, again and again!
Refrain: *Stop-start, stop-start, stop.*
                             (getting gradually slower)

*Substitute another language.

🎓 *Divide the class into the refrain, the conductor, and the various trains.*

Refrain accompaniment

The older children will enjoy performing the rhythms using body percussions and instruments, e.g.

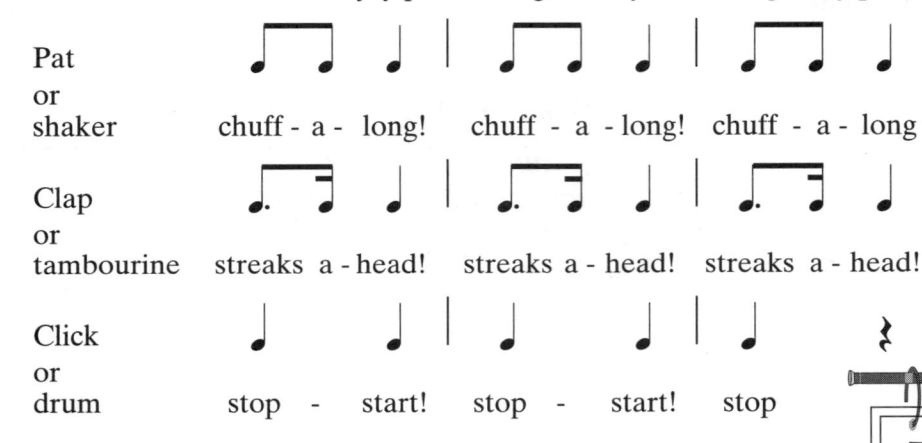

Pat or shaker   chuff - a - long!   chuff - a - long!   chuff - a - long

Clap or tambourine   streaks a - head!   streaks a - head!   streaks a - head!

Click or drum   stop - start!   stop - start!   stop

Children make the sounds separately, then together, to form a rhythmic pattern. Start slowly, accelerating as the train leaves the station. Repeat the pattern, starting quickly and becoming slower as the train enters the station.

The addition of a decrescendo and a crescendo adds to the train soundscape.

Tell the children that...

The Banana Express used to travel along the south coast of Natal. The Orange Express travelled from Durban to Cape Town through the Orange Free State.

A suburban train travels from one part of town to another, stopping at every station.

Horses move at different speeds.

HORSES

Doh: C (Key: C major)

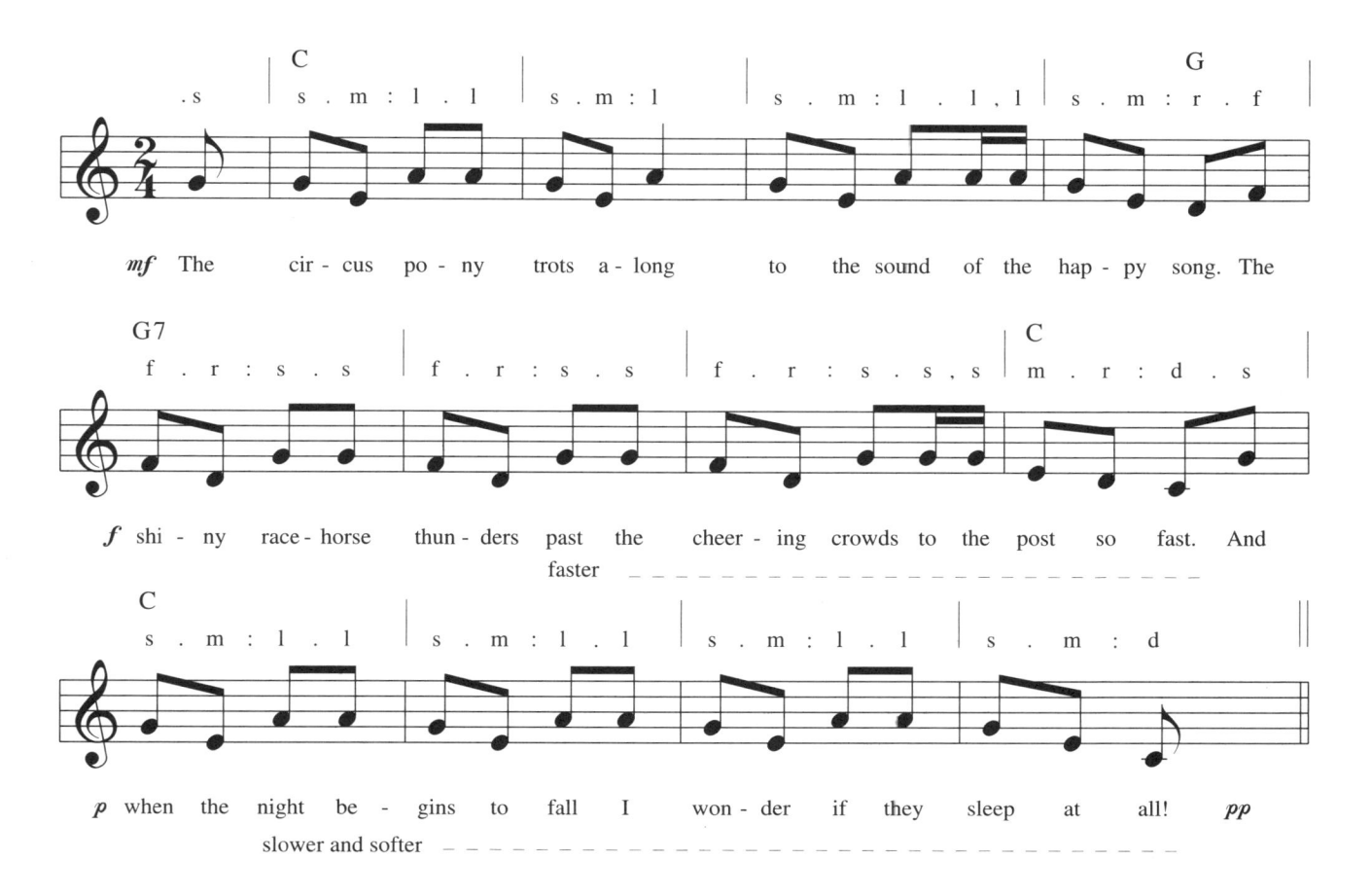

mf The cir-cus po-ny trots a-long to the sound of the hap-py song. The

f shi-ny race-horse thun-ders past the cheer-ing crowds to the post so fast. And
faster — — — — —

p when the night be-gins to fall I won-der if they sleep at all! *pp*
slower and softer — — — —

Sound effects

Encourage the children to create 'horsey' sounds.

1. Sit down and make trotting sounds with your feet or by patting hands on laps:
   trot - trot

2. Do horses 'thunder'? Children try making thunder noises with their feet. They do sound like thunder when they gallop quickly!

3. Try tongue-clicking to depict the sound of horses' hooves, changing speed according to the words.

4. Stamp the feet for thunder sounds, then make softer and slower sounds and finally no sound at all when the horses fall asleep.

Staccato and legato

A squirrel's life includes staccato and legato sounds.
Think of all the fun we'd miss if we slept all winter!

A SQUIRREL'S LIFE

Doh: D (Key: D Major)

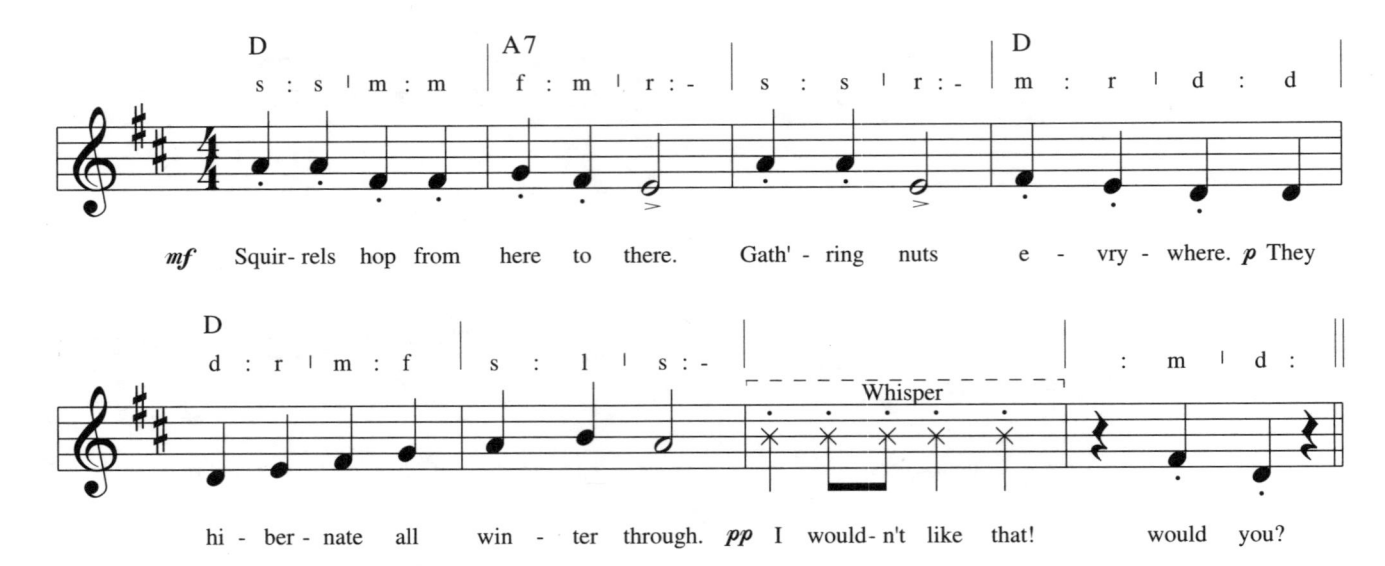

mf Squir-rels hop from here to there. Gath'-ring nuts e-vry-where. *p* They hi-ber-nate all win-ter through. *pp* I would-n't like that! would you?

Accompaniment (xylophone)

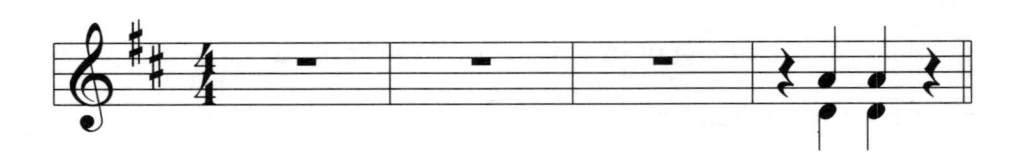

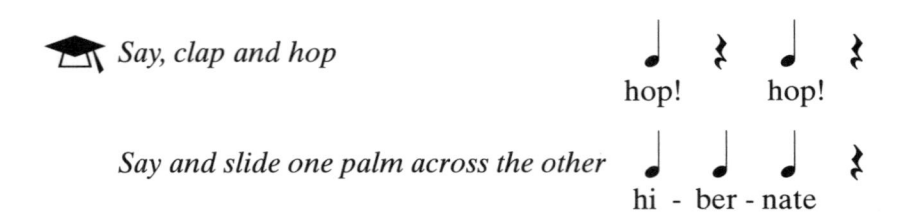

Hop hop

Say, clap and hop
hop! hop!

Say and slide one palm across the other
hi - ber - nate

Let's be . . . SQUIRRELS

Let our hands 'hop' and 'hibernate':

Bars 1 to 4	Children pat their arms, chests or head lightly to the ♩ beat, as if hopping (staccato).
Bars 5 and 6	Move the hand smoothly (legato) along the other arm.
Bar 7	Clap the rhythmic pattern softly and staccato.
Bar 8	Clap the rhythmic pattern loudly and staccato.

The teacher sings and the children act.

Bars 1 to 4	Hop.
Bars 5 and 6	Curl up, as if asleep.
Bars 7 and 8	Sit up, hands on hips and stamp

♩ ♩
would you

Tell the children that . . .

Squirrels play in the Gardens in Cape Town. Some people are lucky enough to have squirrels in their own gardens.

The snake slides smoothly (legato) and also makes a legato hissing sound.

Slang (Afrikaans)

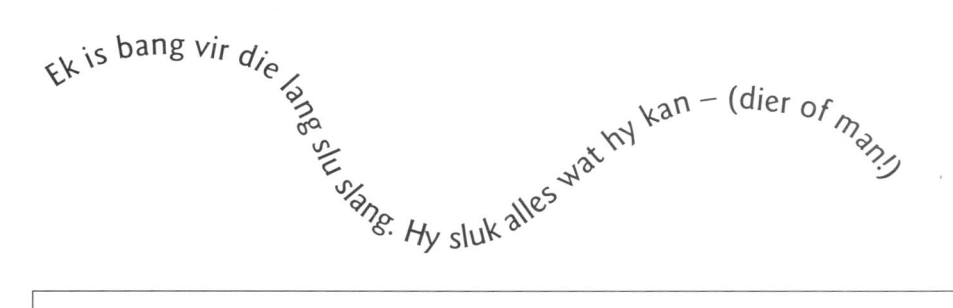

Ek is bang vir die lang slu slang. Hy sluk alles wat hy kan – (dier of man!)

Let's be . . . SNAKES

The teacher says the poem. The children lie on the floor, hissing.

Slide the palms of each hand past the other, as in clashing of cymbals. The hand sliding along the opposite arm or the legs also make a 'ss' sound.

Slide the palms across the skin of the drumhead.

Shake the shakers for a rattlesnake.

Encourage the children to invent their own sounds.

If you touch a porcupine quill, you'll move your hand in a quick staccato way!

PORCUPINE

In a quick, detached way
Doh: G (Key: G major)

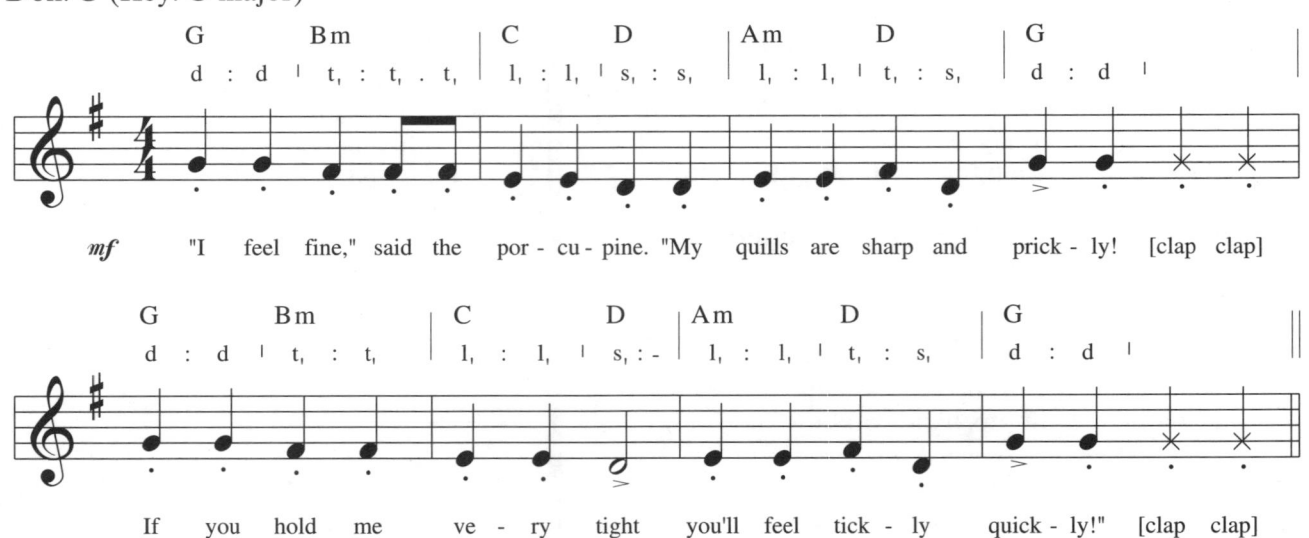

mf "I feel fine," said the por-cu-pine. "My quills are sharp and prick-ly! [clap clap]

If you hold me ve-ry tight you'll feel tick-ly quick-ly!" [clap clap]

Echo effects

Bars 4 and 8   Clap   𝄽 𝄽 ♩ ♩

These notes may be stamped, snapped or clicked, or played on a woodblock or claves.

Words must be said with clear diction as if pricked by 'quills'. This is good practice for agility of lips and tongue.

Tell the children that...

1. Quills are rather like toothpicks. Stick toothpicks into an apple and make your own porcupine. Is your porcupine cuddly or prickly?
2. Sing the song for the children. Ask them to listen carefully. Do they hear the same melody repeated?
3. The children choose from their collection of paper or cardboard shapes two that are the same shape to represent both phrases, e.g. sharp shapes to represent quills.

Loud and soft

Sing, getting softer, so that the baby will fall asleep.

THULA MNTWANA
(Zulu traditional)

Doh: C (Key: C pentatonic)

```
| s : m | s : m . m | s : m . l | s : m | s : m | s : m . m | s . s : m . l | s : m ||
```

p Thu - la mntwa - na, u - ma - ma a - ke - kho. U - yo - then - ga, Ma swi- di am - to - ti!

Ostinato accompaniment

All combinations of the pentatonic scale sound well together.

Let's be . . . THE BABY

One child cries, loudly then . . . gradually softer (decrescendo) until the singing calms him or her to sleep!

Be quiet, my baby (Translated from Zulu)

Be quiet, my baby!
Mother has gone
To buy you sweets.

Echo each bar very softly.

LALA SANA (Xhosa)

Gently
Doh: C (Key: C major)

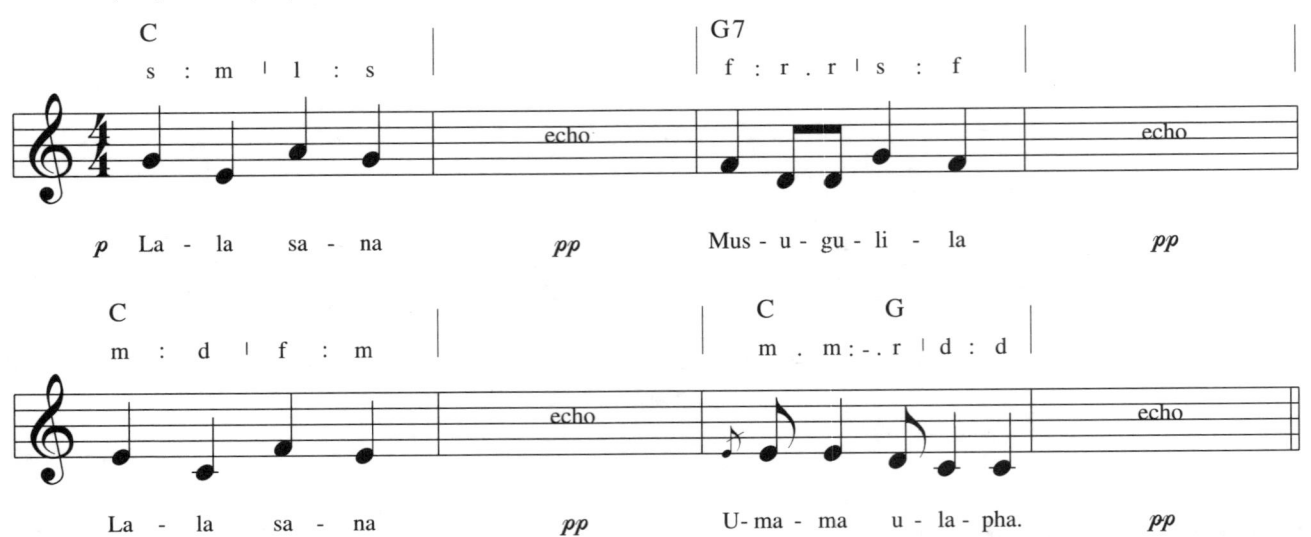

C		G7	
s : m	l : s	f : r . r	s : f

p La - la sa - na *pp* Mus - u - gu - li - la *pp* (echo)

C		C	G
m : d	f : m	m m :- . r	d : d

La - la sa - na *pp* U - ma - ma u - la - pha. *pp* (echo)

Sleep my baby (Translated from Xhosa)

Sleep, my baby
Don't cry,
Sleep, my baby
Your mother is here!

A bulldozer makes a loud sound.

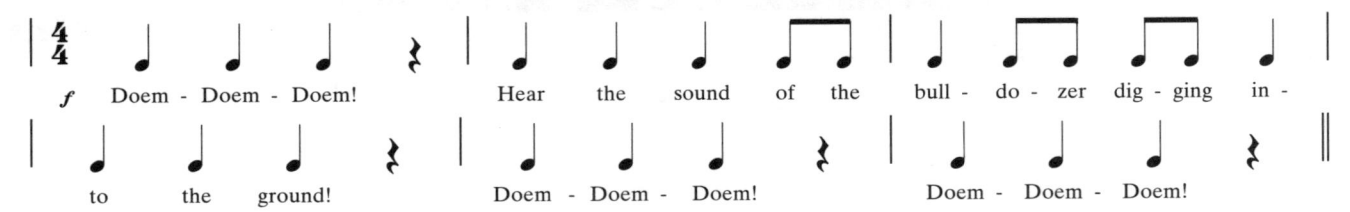

THE BULLDOZER'S SONG

f Doem - Doem - Doem! | Hear the sound of the bull - do - zer dig - ging in -
to the ground! | Doem - Doem - Doem! | Doem - Doem - Doem!

Sound effects

Bars 1, 5 and 6
Drum   Doem-doem-doem

Ostinato accompaniment (claves)

Claves   bull - do - zer   or   doem   doem

The speech pattern may be said by two groups.
Group A   Say bars 1, 5 and 6.
Group B   Say bars 2, 3 and 4.

A loud song to wake you up.

TSOHA! TSOHA!
(Sesotho)

Brightly
Doh: C (Key: C major)

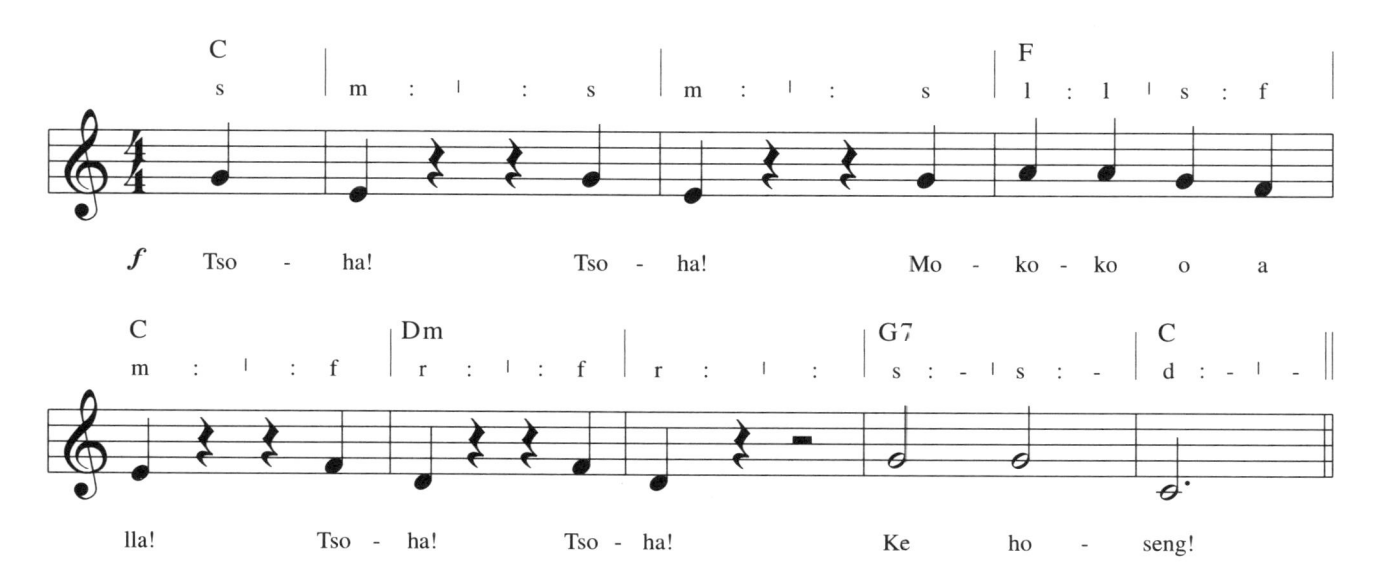

C				F	
s	m : l : s	m : l : s	l : l	s : f	

f Tso - ha!   Tso - ha!   Mo - ko - ko   o   a

C	Dm		G7	C
m : l : f	r : l : f	r : l : —	s : — l s : —	d : — l —

lla!   Tso - ha!   Tso - ha!   Ke   ho - seng!

Wake up! Wake up! *(Translated from Sesotho)*

Wake up! Wake up!
The cock is crowing.
Wake up! Wake up!
It is morning.

Introduction and coda

Children make 'crowing sounds' before and after the poem.

Glossary

MUSICAL TERMS AND SIGNS

𝄐   – pause. Hold the note a little longer than normal.

♩.   – staccato. A detached note.

♩>   – accent. Emphasise the note by playing it louder.

♪   – crushed note. Played very quickly, almost with the next note.

:‖   – repeat.

D.C. al Fine   – from the beginning to the word 'Fine' (end).

glissando   – melodic percussion. Slide the beater from the highest to the lowest notes, or vice versa.

tremolo   – triangle. Quick repeated playing.

ostinato   – a repeated pattern.

Dynamics

p	– piano	soft
pp	– pianissimo	very soft
mp	– mezzopiano	fairly soft
f	– forte	loud
ff	– fortissimo	very loud
mf	– mezzoforte	fairly loud
$<$	– crescendo	becoming gradually louder
$>$	– decrescendo	becoming gradually softer

Form

bar   – a measure of musical time. When counting bars, bar 1 is the first complete bar.

coda   – a short ending.

Music theory

Major scales

C major

C D E F G A B C

PRIMARY CHORDS

Chord I   C - E - G
Chord IV   F - A - C
Chord V   G - B - D
Chord V_7 G - B - D - F

C major has no key-signature.

F major

F G A B♭ C D E F

PRIMARY CHORDS

Chord I   F - A - C
Chord IV   B♭ - D - F
Chord V   C - E - G
Chord V_7 C - E - G - B♭

The key-signature of F major is B♭.
Xylophone: Replace B with B♭.

G major

G A B C D E F♯ G

PRIMARY CHORDS

Chord I   G - B - D
Chord IV   C - E - G
Chord V   D - F♯ - A
Chord V_7 D - F♯ - A - C

The key signature of G major is F♯.
Xylophone: Replace F with F♯.

D major

D E F♯ G A B C♯ D

PRIMARY CHORDS

Chord I   D - F♯ - A
Chord IV   G - B - D
Chord V   A - C♯ - E
Chord V_7 A - C♯ - E - G

The key-signature of D major is F♯, C♯.
Xylophone: Replace F and C with F♯ and C♯.

A major

A B C# D E F# G# A

PRIMARY CHORDS

Chord I   A - C# - E
Chord IV   D - F# - A
Chord V   E - G# - B
Chord V_7 E - G# - B - D

The key-signature of A major is F#, C#, G#.
Xylophone: Replace F and C with F# and C#. Remove G if there is no G# bar to replace it.

Bb major

B♭ C D E♭ E G A B♭

PRIMARY CHORDS

Chord I   B♭ - D - F
Chord IV   E♭ - G - B♭
Chord V   F - A - C
Chord V_7 F - A - C - E♭

The key-signature of B♭ major is B♭, E♭.
Xylophone: Replace B with B♭. Remove E if there is no E♭ bar with which to replace it.

Harmonic minor scales

A minor

A B C D E F G# A

PRIMARY CHORDS

Chord I   A - C - E
Chord IV   D - F - A
Chord V   E - G# - B
Chord V_7 E - G# - B - D

A minor is 'related' to C major. It has no key signature. However, the 7th note is raised from G to G#. The G# does not appear in the key signature but is written each time it occurs.
Xylophone: Replace G with G#.
The A minor songs in *Take Note* do not require a G# as the instrument does not usually include a G# note.

D minor

D E F G A B♭ C# D

PRIMARY CHORDS

Chord I   D - F - A
Chor IV   G - B♭ - D
Chord V   A - C# - E
Chord V_7 A - C# - E - G

D minor is 'related' to F major. The key-signature is B♭, and the 7th note, C, is raised to C#. The C# is written out each time it appears.

('Die olifant' is written in D melodic minor, descending – D C# B♭ A G F E D.)

E minor

E F# G A B C D# E

PRIMARY CHORDS

Chord I   E - G - B
Chord IV   A - C - E
Chord V   B - D# - F#
Chord V_7 B - D# - F# - A

E minor is 'related' to G major. The key-signature is F#, and the 7th note, D, is raised to D#. The D# is written out each time it appears.

G minor

G A B♭ C D E♭ F# G

PRIMARY CHORDS

Chord I   G - B♭ - D
Chord IV   C - E♭ - G
Chord V   D - F# - A
Chord V_7 D - F# - A - C

G minor is 'related' to B♭ major. The key-signature is B♭, E♭, and the 7th note, F is raised to F#. The F# is written out each time it appears.
('The whale' is written in G melodic minor, ascending – G A B♭ C D E♮ F# G.)

Pentatonic scale (five notes)

C D E G A

All notes, individually, or in combination, sound well together.

Guitar chords

⌒ Barre chords. First finger holds down the strings.
x Do not play these strings.

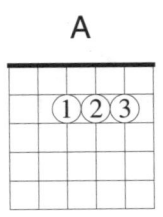

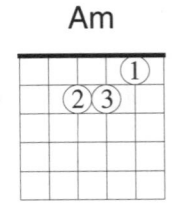

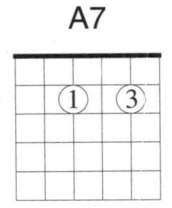

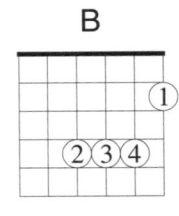

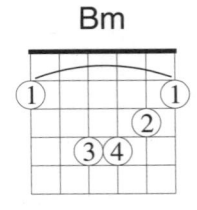

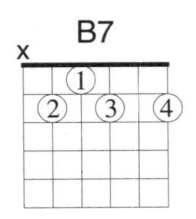

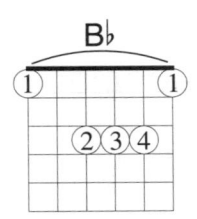

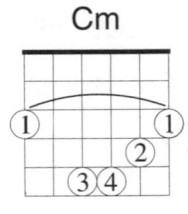

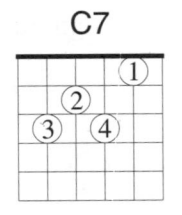

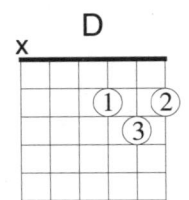

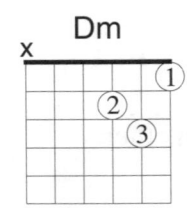

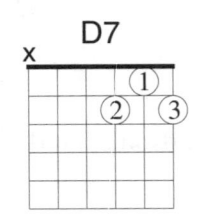

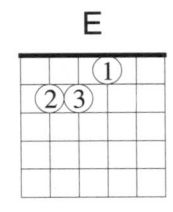

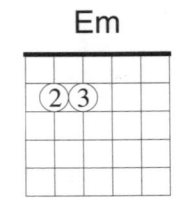

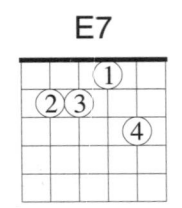

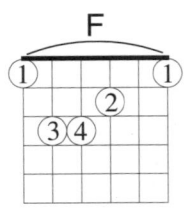

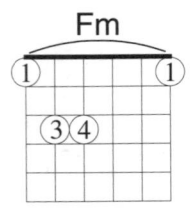

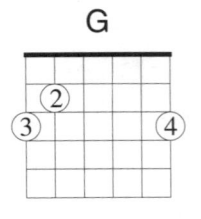

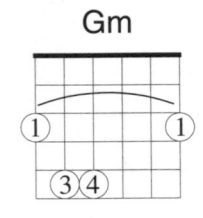

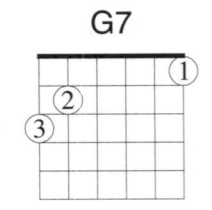